THEATRE

THE GOOD, THE BAD, THE BEAUTIFUL

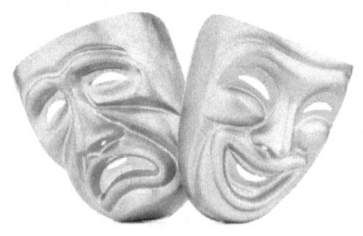

JAY HORNE

Published by Jay Horne
Cover Design by Sarah Foster from Sprinkles On Top Studios
Formatting by Elaine York/Allusion Graphics, LLC/
Publishing & Book Formatting, www.allusiongraphics.com

DEDICATION

This story of theatre, and all its aspects—history, character, memorization, impromptu, auditioning, directing, tech and just good fun—is dedicated to Vivian Kirsch Horne: the woman who first got me involved with theatre, and worked with me side by side.

Thank you.

All my love,
Jay

Jay's Theatre Adventures

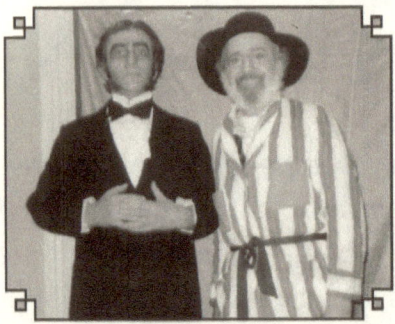

Jay as Mr. Sowerberry in Oliver!

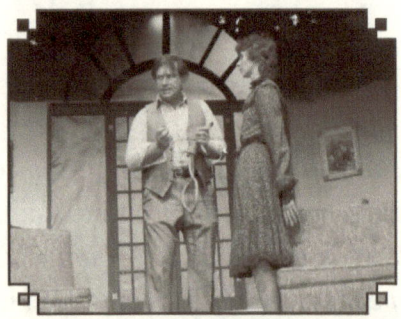

Jay as Sir Lawrence Wargrave in
Ten Little Indians.

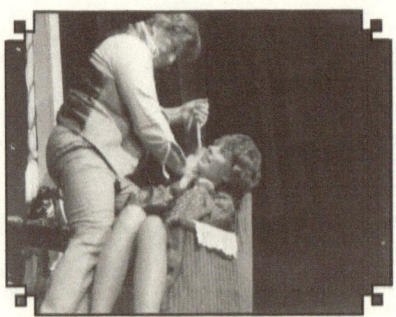

Jay in action as Sir Lawrence
Wargrave in Ten Little Indians.

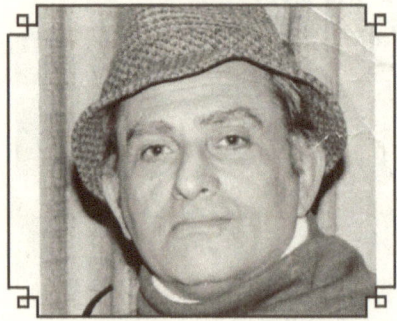

Jay as Sir Lawrence Wargrave in
Ten Little Indians.

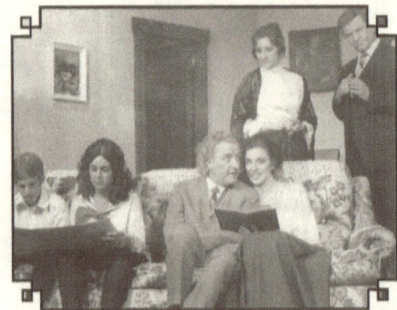

Jay as Nat Miller in Ah,
Wilderness!

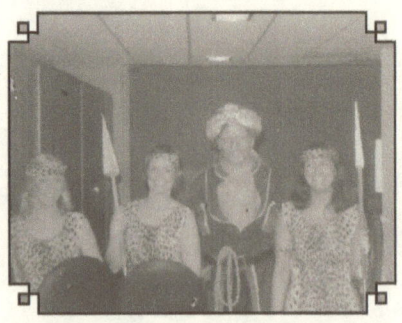

Jay as Jawan in Kismet.

Jay's Theatre Adventures

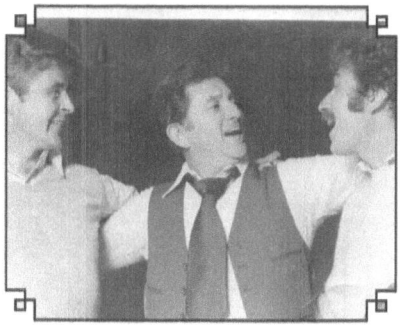

Jay as Willy Loman in
Death of a Salesman.

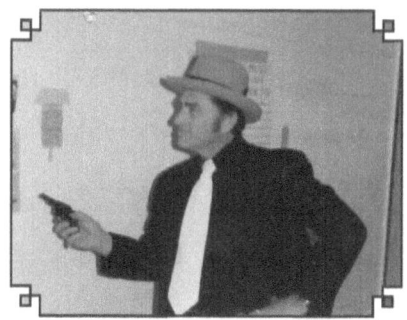

Jay as Carmine Vespucci
in The Ritz.

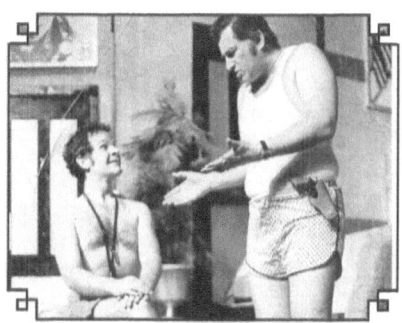

Jay as Carmine Vespucci
in The Ritz.

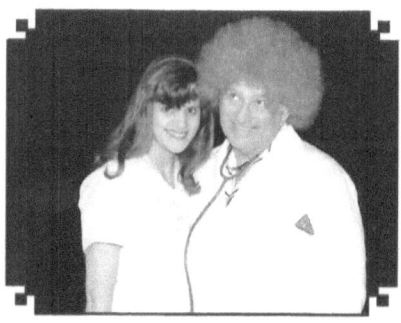

Jay as Dr. Klockenmeyer in The
Sunshine Boys.

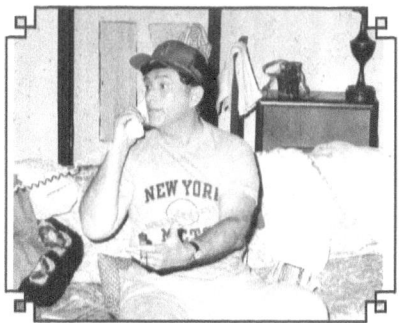

Jay as Oscar Madison
in The Odd Couple.

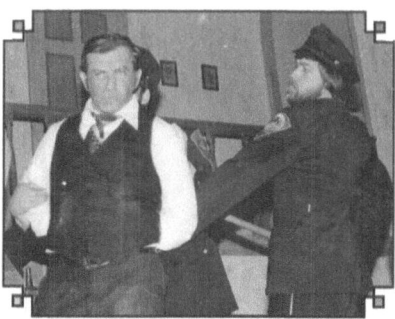

Jay as Jonathan Brewster in
Arsenic and Old Lace.

TABLE OF CONTENTS

INTRODUCTION

My experience with the theatre covers over forty-one years. During that time, I was involved with close to 315 productions, either as a director (82 shows), tech director, actor (150 shows) or producer, and have served on ten theatre boards as president, vice-president, business manager, tech director and play-reading chairman.

This was all done in New York, New England, Chicago and Arizona. I have received numerous state, regional and theatre awards in the "best of" categories. In addition, I attended a community college in the Chicago area to study all aspects of theatre for three and a half years. I was selected out of the class of forty-two as the outstanding student in all phases of theatre.

Following, I was offered an assistant professor position to teach theatre.

In addition, I have reviewed theatre shows in the New York area, New England, Chicago and Arizona for local newspapers, magazines and, now, my own blog.

I'd like to give particular notice to two theatres in Arizona that deserve special recognition: Arizona Broadway Theatre and Theater Works. Arizona Broadway Theatre, or ABT, is a professional dinner theatre, and is the best example of an outstanding dinner theatre. Not only do they offer high-quality dining, but superb theatrical shows as well. ABT is the living embodiment of what good theatre is all about – it works for all, and welcomes others into its family atmosphere. Theater Works, with its strong, professional attitude, takes on shows that other well-known theatres won't due to the difficulties with tech and tough acting requirements. The theatre is in its 30th year of outstanding shows and special performances. Both of these excellent theatres are in Peoria, Arizona.

I have also enjoyed teaching youth and adult theatre classes at various theatres in the above cities.

I wrote this book not to lecture, but rather to offer a guide for amateurs or beginners interested in getting involved with theatre. Regardless of the area of theatre you choose to enter, I say to all, you have to have a passion and a true desire to do it. If it's just a means to an end, do not do it!

I hope by reading this book you'll understand that it can be a very rewarding and uplifting experience.

Yours for theatre,
Jay Horne

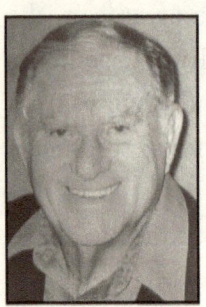

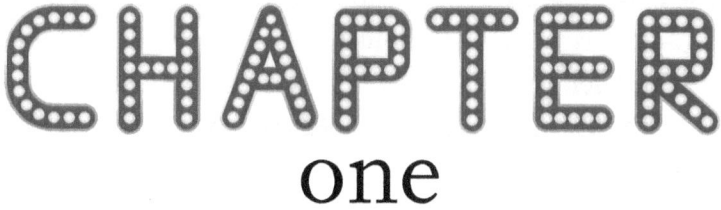

one

The History & Origins of Theatre

Webster's dictionary definition of theater or theatre: any place where events take place; A – The dramatic arts. B – The theatrical world.

If I may, before we get into what will follow, I would like to quote something Shakespeare once said, "All the world's a stage, and all the men and women merely players: they have their exits and their entrances..."

The record of ancient history proves that miming, dancing and similar forms have been popular for thousands of years. Among certain races, important events are still celebrated with ritual dances and speeches, which have changed, in some cases, very little since the Stone Age. It is from such limited origins that a great art has developed. You can say it began with ancient man during the Stone Age with the drawings on the walls of their caves, and later when they discovered fire. Around the fire, they would relay to their fellow tribal members the adventures they experienced.

There have been many expressions of drama, from the humanities of the Greek theatre, which consisted of amphitheaters of stone in a semi-circle. There, they performed tales of great Greek heroes and their tragedies.

The Romans in the days of the Emperors Nero and Caesar also had a form of theatre, usually at the coliseum in Rome where chariot races and man-against-man combat (called Gladiators), as well as man against wild beasts.

By the way, man very rarely won.

These performances, in my opinion, were called theatre of the ridiculous; it was all to entertain the rabid crowds, the deranged emperors and their guests.

Many of the first actors, in the modern sense, were unpaid members of the trade guilds who gave performances in their spare time. This was during the Middle Ages, and in many cases the plays were based on folklore and performed without scripts or many rehearsals; only the bare outline of the story was known to the actors, who improvised their parts.

During the 16th and 17th centuries, masques and plays became popular diversions for the upper classes. This was partly because of the need for some form of entertainment to take the place of jousting and tournaments. As the power of the guilds began to decline, and a large number of public holidays, formerly holy days, ceased to be recognized, amateur theatrical works gradually became limited to those with ample wealth and leisure.

During this period, there evolved many great playwrights and classic plays that remain known to the present day. Of course, the Bard of England William Shakespeare, who wrote many great plays, such as "A Midsummer Night's Dream" and "Twelfth Night" – one of the most amusing of Shakespeare's comedies. Other great plays were "The Taming Of The Shrew," "Romeo and Juliet," "Hamlet," "Othello," "Macbeth" and many other outstanding works written in the late 16th and early 17th centuries. He wrote a total of forty-two classics that will remain with us through eternity.

It was about this same time that opera came about. The title opera covers a multitude of theatrical forms, from the Wagnerian epic to the popular performances better classified as musical comedy.

There are two main kinds of opera: those that are songs, duets, quartets etc., and those in which spoken words connect the different passages. It may be noted that it is either half singing and have speaking, or the explanatory passages between songs.

The original, or basic form of opera was based on the Florentine Camerata of the 16th century. This was a musical setting of a Greek or

Latin drama. During the 17th century, the fame of such early Italian composers such as Monteverdi, led nearly every European court and cultural center to attempt to form an operatic group. In France, as early as 1761, there was a flourish in Royal Academy to encourage opera and ballet.

The Germans and northern Europeans were not at first as adept as the French and Italians at composition and performance of operas; however, by the middle of the 18th century, two great German composers, Gluck and Mozart, changed things by turning a considerable part of their attention to this type of music.

Operas of the 17th and 18th centuries, including the English operas of Porlek and Handel, commonly known as romantic opera, began to make its appearance.

This was typical by Rozzini, Donizetti and Verdi in Italy, Weber in Germany, Auber and Gounod in France, as well as Balfe and Wallace in the British Isles.

Finally, Richard Wagner, who tried to place opera on the highest peak of artistic achievement, attempted this new trend. At first, the Wagnerian style was not always met with enthusiasm—for many years, in fact. In later years, Wagner's works received the measure of popularity it deserved, ensuring fame for one of the greatest original artist of the 19th century, as well as all time.

During the 18th century, the Irish seemed to have a genius for producing writers of first class comedy, among them being such giants as Bernard Shaw, Oliver Goldsmith, Oscar Wilde and Richard Sherman. Ibsen who wrote "Peer Gynt" is an excellent example of expressionistic drama, at which Scandinavian writers of the 19th century excelled. It offers plenty of humor, poetry and dramatic scope for play reading.

Ballet, a performance of dancing as a full or part-time entertainment, at present time, is a spectacle without words. At first, it was popular in Italy and France, although it should be noted its complex rituals have little in common with the dancing and miming of mummers and acrobats. Until the 18th century, masks, stiff clothes and long skirts hampered ballet dancers. Camargo, the great exponent of the times, challenged these regulations. During the period of the French revolution, Noverre, who introduced skin fitting tights worn beneath light skirts, made other reforms.

Toward the end of the 19th century, ballet became popular in Russia. Here, as in France and Italy, it got the full support of the nobility. The cooperation of Petipa, the French director of dancing, and the Russian composer Tchaikovsky introduced the grand scale—three act ballets such as "The Nutcracker" and "Swan Lake."

Although this form of ballet is still one of the most popular types of entertainment, it went through a period of dullness and sterility. It took an American dancer, Isadora Duncan, to help revitalize the ballet by touring Western Europe and Russia with new ideas and schemes.

Her beliefs were based on a considerable measure of barefoot dancing, the revived importance of early Grecian ideals and the emphasis of solo performances.

The first principle of the theatre should be to provide the version rather than instruction.

Although some great plays have been used as a vehicle for moral and political theories, even these can fail to make an impression when the play lacks interest, or the parts are poorly acted.

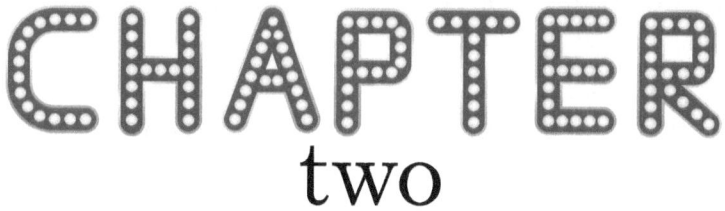

two

Initial Arrangements

Start by finding a producer. When a group is being formed it should always include someone with a definite aptitude for production.

Other key people, such as a stage manager and lighting specialists, can be added at a slightly later stage, but it is essential to start with the producer.

If the circle forming the nucleus of an amateur group does not include such an expert with previous experience, an attempt should be made to find one. This is because the producer needs to be consulted with in regard to the choice of a play and initial casting.

Let's get into some of the basic information of the key people that will help you put together a production.

Specialists:

Specialists, such as electricians and stage carpenters, may be encouraged to join the group on the understanding their work will be useful experience.

Stage Manager:

The stage manager should work in close relationship with the producer, who is, in many ways, his or her nearest counterpart. The stage manager is responsible for making sure actors are in place and arrangement of furniture and scenery is set. The property master, electrician, wardrobe mistress and other specialists take direct orders from this important person.

Property Master:

It is the duty of this person to look after the furniture and scenery, which are known in the theatrical jargon as "properties" or "props." This person should keep up-to-date lists of all items in their care, and check them for loss or damage. A good property master is also handy to make any last-minute repairs.

Wardrobe Mistress:

This person usually supervises the dressers and is in sole charge of the costumes. It is his or her duty to see that all of the actors and actresses are correctly fitted in the costumes for which they are intended. For this purpose, the wardrobe mistress should have the latest measurements of all members of the cast. If the costumes are hired or borrowed, the wardrobe mistress must see that all pieces are packed and dispatched with care upon completion of the show's run.

Dressers:

Most importantly actors or actresses almost expect to have someone help them get dressed and prepped for a performance. The presence of a dresser is appreciated most when the play is performed with historical costumes, or elaborate pieces contain hooks and tapes. A good dresser should always know when to have the right costume or accessory on hand, as delays in dressing rooms may spoil the whole routine and timeline of the play.

Stage Carpenter:

The work of the stage carpenter almost speaks for itself. The person in this role is often taken for granted to such an extent that people forget his or her importance in the grand scheme of a production. The work should not really be classified a duty, but also a necessity. The work must be of sound craftsmanship, as failure in this respect may lead to accidents.

Prompters:

This specialist follows the script at both rehearsals and, in some cases, public performances in order to assist or prompt those who have forgotten their lines. The prompter usually stands on the left side of the stage. He or she should have a clear voice, which must not betray any accent or irritation. The prompter also signals for the raising and lowering of the curtain, as designated by the stage manager. The responsibilities of prompting call for deep concentration and self-control. There is always a tendency to let the mind wander if the actors seem confident, and if that happens awkward pauses may occur when the unexpected happens. The quotation of the sentence following the pause should be enough to furnish the actor with the clue to the forgotten lines. The prompter must be reliable as the role also requires checking the pre-arranged times for intervals and breaks. In today's theatre, some of these duties may be absorbed into the stage manager's role as well.

Call Person:

Often called the prompter's assistant, a person in this role warns actors and actresses outside their dressing rooms shortly before they are due to make an appearance. They can do this by knocking and calling at least two minutes before the required entrance. Again, in theatres with modern technology, or a large crew, the stage manager may perform this role and delegate a number of duties to an assistant.

Some final thoughts on how a good producer is crucial to a production.

Most of the individual responsibilities for a play depend on the producer. Too often, the praise or blame is credited to actors or scriptwriters, while the producer must be content with only scant acknowledgement.

Much to the contrary, the producer is not only the coordinating factor between the various elements of his craft; he or she is also a foil between actors and authors.

Like most forms of artistic expression, there will always be disagreement or artistic differences. Ever since plays have been written and produced, there has been a certain amount of disagreement between writer and interpreter as to the way in which parts should be performed.

CHAPTER
three

Common Terms Relating to the Theatre

The following terms are explained to help someone find his or her way about the theatre, and enable them to approach a professional standard of appreciation and performance.

Act: A play is divided into a certain number of acts, which are subdivided into scenes.

Act Drop: The act drop is a curtain that closes off the stage from the auditorium at the end of each act.

Apron Stage: This is a stage that projects into the auditorium.

Back Cloth: A flat canvas at the back of the stage that is painted to imitate scenery, architecture and the like.

Book Wing: A flat place in the wings that can be made to revolve by means of a wheel and spindle. Or, in more modern theatre houses, using stage tech programming.

Blackout: The lights on the stage cut out to achieve the effect of sudden darkness.

Brace: The diagonal support that holds a flat in place from behind.

Brace Weight: A weight fitted onto the foot of the brace to keep it steady. This is a quicker method of securing flats than screwing them to the floor or wall.

Burlesque: A satirical form of stage entertainment.

Cloudings: Borders painted to imitate a cloud effect or skyscape.

Cue: The moment an actor recognizes as the beginning of his or her lines, or when they should begin to speak them.

Curtain raiser: A short play, often a comedy, produced before a longer play appearing on the same program.

Drop: Scenery lowered on the stage from a grid above the stage area.

Epilogue: A short scene at the end of the play in which the main characters may appear to sum up the developments of the play.

Flie: The space above the stage. This area often dictates, to some level, the height or effects that can be used on stage, especially the simulation of flying.

Fit Up: A temporary setting.

Green Room: The actors' common room.

Legs: Curtains or lengths of unframed canvas.

Quick Change Room: A small cubicle near the wings, offstage, used for quick changes of costume and makeup between scenes.

Rake: The angle of the stage. Most theatres rake their stages, sometimes with what are called fox wedges, at an angle of one inch to two feet.

Scene Bay: A space behind the stage for storing scenery.

Sloat: A moving but hidden part of the stage that conveys actors from one part to another.

Tragic Carpet: A carpet on which actors fall when struck down by illness or death on the stage.

These are just some of the terms used in theatre to get you started on your journey to discover theatre. As you can see, it's a language that is commonly used by people only in the theatre world.

CHAPTER
four

Types of Productions

There are many types of productions aside from the conventional play. These may include ballet, opera, musical comedy, pantomime and variety programs.

In choosing the production most suitable for, let's say, an amateur production, the talents of the members have to be taken into account. As a rule, this means ballet and opera are unsuitable. Both are highly specialized entertainments that require hard training beyond the scope of most beginners.

It may be said that operatic societies exist in all parts of the country, but this is a merely singular distinction. Such groups rarely attempt a full-scale opera, and have confined themselves to later works, such as musical comedy. However, even in lighter music it is advisable to have first-rate performers. Few things seem more distasteful than music given without ability or instruction.

Although skill is required for straight acting, this seems to be of a particular order, which is not so blatant when it fails to be a success. There is always something about a good straight play that will hold the attention of an audience, however poor the acting may seem.

On the other hand, music is wholly evaluated by weak interpretation.

Pantomime and variety have some problems in common, but there are also essential differences.

One plus in favor of pantomime is that, however varied the program, there is no need for a master of ceremonies or chairman to introduce the performers. Thus, the need for writing witty and meaningful scripts for the master of ceremonies—always a difficult task—is avoided.

A frequent struggle in organizing a "variety" performance is staying true to the name, in other words making the program varied.

Singing and other musical acts are always popular, and often constitute the main background of the entertainment, but that should not be overdone.

Comedians and novelty acts are the jam in the sandwich, but even the best jam loses its flavor if the bread is too thick.

When asked to arrange for either pantomime or variety, a factor to be considered is local preference, if any, and current industry popularity.

Different types of performances, and even varieties of musical instruments, have fluctuations of entertainment value. However, in attempting to keep up-to-date, avoid the possibility of being too far in advance of the audience, as this mistake will lead to even wider misunderstanding and lack of sympathy.

Running ahead in this way is a frequent blunder, especially in some more "country" or rural areas where people are not so much under the influence of television and movies.

The modern pantomime is often described as little more than a children's story over which variety acts have been super imposed.

The plot typically ceases to be the most important part of the show, but this does not mean it can be neglected. It has to be both topical and convincing, yet rooted in fairytale tradition at the same time.

By a strange paradox, the audience, while looking for new jokes and situations, will not tolerate a departure from the background atmosphere or the employment of stock characters.

Pantomime has become an institution almost on a national scale, and must be treated conventionally. One of the main disadvantages in this is that although variety and straight plays can be given throughout the year, pantomime is usually kept to the period between the end of December and Easter.

Scripts for novice pantomimes are usually written by members of the performing company, and are often the result of a joint effort.

As pantomimes change each year, there is considerably little point in publishing this type of script on a large scale, making them difficult to find in printed form.

It should be remembered that when using songs or tunes from other shows, the licensing companies that own the rights, such as Samuel French, Dramatic Publishers, Music Theatre International (MTI) or others, must give permission to the theatre and/or performer.

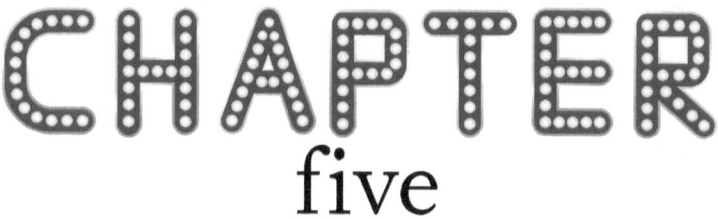

CHAPTER
five

Features of Acting

The most important aspect once you have been selected to play a role is characterization.

One must truly become, and take on the persona and mannerisms of, the role as portrayed by the playwright and director in order to be believable to an audience and fellow castmates.

Good acting should be, in most senses, a convincing reproduction of life. The performance fails to have any meaning or authenticity when only one or two actors in the cast are concentrating on their parts.

The Supporting Cast

Overacting is a common and deplorable fault, but what might be termed "underacting" is even worse. The actor who speaks his or her lines, and then relapses into wooden immobility is of no more value to the production than a robot or a recording.

The supporting actors should not draw special attention to themselves, but everything they do must be normal and unobtrusive. These actions include things such as lighting a pipe or turning the pages of a book. Those small but important actions required of the supporting actor must be worked out at rehearsals until they are perfectly timed and adjusted.

Unfortunately, the stage directions normally appearing with the script do not always offer notes on these matters. On the plus side, this gives the small-part player a chance to improvise, which can help improve overall technique and enhance creative abilities. However, great care should be taken to avoid being over absorbed in minor duties, as this could lead to missing cues.

Appearing On The Stage

When acting in public the first few times, appearing on the stage can create a fear of, or actual, failing; this is usually a result of a lack in confidence.

That is one of the main reasons why important or leading roles should only be attempted after many experiences in doing minor parts.

However enthusiastic, to some, the prospect of standing on stage in front of utter strangers is terrifying. But, there is no need to sound the alarm as people do not (usually) throw tomatoes at amateurs—at least I haven't experienced this occurrence in over 41 years of involvement with theatre.

The audiences' reaction to moments of error on stage is usually one of sympathy toward those whose mistakes are due to nervousness or inexperience as opposed to carelessness.

Forgetting the audience and keeping to a strict routine of action that has been determined by the creative team is usually how one can acquire self-confidence.

A tip: move and breathe as though you were performing these simple functions in your home.

Think of the matter at hand, and not of what others may be thinking.

If the inexperienced are able to conduct themselves according to these simple rules, they need not fear public reaction.

Character Parts

Those who play leading roles can be divided into two major groups. These include actors who can assume any role as a result of application and study, and those who are particularly suited, by virtue of their talents, to play a limited range of parts.

The first category may be subdivided between the person who conforms every part to his or her own image, and the actor who loses his identity in the adoption of a role. Apropos for the former type, theatre and cinemagoers may remember the fine performances of James Cagney.

This actor could interpret George M. Cohen in "Yankee Doodle Dandy" or the maniacal killer Cody in "White Heat" with almost equal skill, but there was never any chance of personal deception. The expressions and movements would be those of a great songwriter or a crazed killer; however, the actor in question managed his part so well people would go to see him as much for his own sake as for the plays and movies in which he appeared.

The amateur is well advised to try a distinctly different interpretation that falls into the second of the categories.

In this, he suppresses his own character and makes a sincere effort to live the relevant part as a different type of person.

There is thus no similarity between the various roles, so that every part is different and interesting. This does not mean they should adopt such a technique because it is easier than the strictly personal approach, but because it is the only means whereby he can make progress.

The aim should always be to the event of every day life, and re-create his personality on the stage. Although he will not be able to do this as completely as the professional, the later method does not require as much natural skill as the alternative.

Regarding the actor who, for either physical or mental reasons, fits into a conventional part, such an actor is invaluable in the roles he or she takes on, but may be almost useless in other branches.

One can draw such an example from the late great Orson Welles, who had to build an appearance of an austere business mogul in the classic "Citizen Kane."

It does not detract from his talent, or from his wonderful reputation, to say it would have been almost unthinkable to cast him as a clown, prizefighter or a tramp.

CHAPTER
six

Faults – Articulation – Movement

There are worse faults in drama than any previously mentioned. The most despicable of these is known as upstaging, which means an actor tries to detract from the importance of another by drawing attention to himself.

This may be done for motives of jealousy or self-adulation, and takes the form of keeping the actor hidden from the audience by moving in front of him.

In this case, the person to be upstaged is confined to the back or upper part of the stage.

Shouting is another fault common to both amateurs and professionals. Even some actors and some reputed American performers are inclined to cry if they get half the chance. This is because they subscribe, almost unwittingly, to the school of thought that seeks to ban natural performances from the stage.

These misguided people imagine every word and syllable must resound to the back of the auditorium regardless of the tone of voice and how it should be uttered.

An audience expects to hear the whole of the play, and nothing is achieved by muttering a part; however, it is better to seem normal, though inaudible, than to make an unnatural sound.

A person who cannot be heard without shouting has no right to be on stage. It's okay to speak louder on the stage in the correct, or required, circumstances, but not louder than the other actors.

In correct talking, control is maintained without conscious effort, and is the result of effective breathing and keeping mentally cool.

Among movements that appear unsightly on the stage is what is known as the scissor cross. This occurs when two actors set out to cross the stage at the same time and meet halfway. Although this may be exploited in some types of comedy, it looks very odd in a straight play.

Another fault an actor should learn to avoid is the presentation to the audience of a back view for too long of a period. This may be done in embarrassment accidentally, or because the part has been active in the wrong way.

Sadly, many producers are inclined to be dogmatic about this failing, for whatever the reason. There is fundamental soundness to the policy though, as the audience feels they are missing something when they cannot see an actor's face.

Some scenes do demand the actor turn his or her back for at least part of the time, and when this cannot be avoided it must be done with great discretion.

It is a further mistake to stand directly in front of other people on the stage, even without any intention of upstaging. Similarly, an actor should also avoid being too much toward one side of the stage unless directed.

Speech

This is, of necessity, an important feature, but some feel it has been overemphasized in modern times.

The technique of elocution and the effects of correct breathing and posture have turned into hard taskmasters at the time a performer should remain calm.

There are some very elementary rules for normal voice production and good acting.

The first of these deals with stance or posture, as this not only affects the appearance of the body but also the method of speech. Correct speech, like any other physical activity, depends on correct breathing. In the first case, focus on breathing from the lower, rather than the upper, part of your lungs—your diaphragm becomes the source of muscle activity. In this way, there is less strain on the chest and throat and no visible movement of the upper body.

With regard to stance, actors should never slump, lean or lounge about lazily. People who stand about in an undignified manner are usually those who take the path of least resistance, and it is not surprising this should be betrayed by their voices.

The correct posture for straight acting is a normal upright position without too much stiffness or formality. In this way, it is possible to keep the head direct and the shoulders back without imitating a soldier on parade.

Articulation

One of the chief aspects of speech is articulation, but this largely depends on the enunciation of the vowels and correct framing of the consonants. Although a clear and articulate person is more readily understood than one who slurs his speech, there are temptations for the correct deliverers to speak either too quickly or too slowly.

The remedy for these disorders is to keep an even pace, while delivering each word as if it were important. This does not mean the actor must always speak in a vital, somber manner, but they should try to consider adjusting each word according to its significance.

Correct pitch is a matter of speaking in a normal tone. High or overpitching, which is just shouting, is quite unnecessary as previously mentioned.

Dialect

The use of dialect may be regarded as a mixed blessing. While some have a natural tendency to apply this direction, others may seem incapable of understanding its values.

By a strange paradox, the best speakers of unusual dialects are often those with knowledge of correct language. People who have a dialect seem unable to impersonate those from other areas. Some actors take great pains to study dialects, a policy which is commendable.

Movement

Movement is one of the most important parts of good acting; some experts are of the opinion it is even more important than diction itself.

In support of the previous theory, it has been recorded that one of the greatest Shakespearian actors was sometimes inflicted with a speech defect, making him inaudible.

He was once hampered by this weakness during an important scene in "Richard III," but managed to carry on with such eloquent gestures that he was applauded from all sides.

This would not have been possible if the actor concerned had failed to spend as much time practicing movement and mime as he did to verbal utterance.

Few beginners realize it is just as necessary to perfect the movements, as it is to learn the words.

For this reason, most untutored people fall into one of two categories which may be termed "the loose" and "the tight."

Loose actors stand and move in a negligent manner, and often resort to nervous movement, which may be a normal characteristic or taken of stage fright.

The tight actor, determined not to be nervous, is symbolized by the extreme jerkiness of his or her movements, often making them appear more like a puppet than a human being.

Finding a happy medium between extremes is one of an actor's first duties. It entails acting naturally in an artificial manner.

The art of acting, in comparison with other fine arts, does not aim at merely imitating life, but improvising in a select manner.

CHAPTER
seven

Grouping & Awareness

<u>Grouping</u>

Grouping is one of the major problems facing the producer and director when they are coping with a large cast. This has particular meaning for companies that favor musical productions, as in their case chorus work forms such an important part of the program.

The following remarks are intended to correct the more obvious faults.

Sometimes when a number of small-part players enter a set at the same time they often appear like a squad of soldiers detailed for some unpleasant task. Their smiles are artificial smirks in the grin-and-bear-it tradition, and in some cases they even walk in step and file.

These may seem very simple faults, but they are also common and difficult to avoid.

It is a well-known fact a group of people assembled for the same purpose tends to lose identity. The average election mob or out-of-control football crowd are examples of this factor. This is not because they are without will and ideas of their own, but because their true expressions are hindered by nervousness or boredom.

In the former case, which is the most usual among amateurs, the actor enters the stage hardly daring to put one foot in front of another for fear of drawing attention. Then, with a sudden burst of realization, the suspect of the fear remembers they are on stage for the purpose of being noticed.

After such an awakening, the mind is so disturbed that nothing is seen with clarity and good sense. The actor knows something must be done, so they waive their arms or move their legs in the same manner as the nearest neighbor.

When such an attitude is repeated by other members of the cast, the results are as might be expected—the epitome of dullness and uniformity.

The way to avoid the perplexity of mind, which is the root of nervousness, is to insist on well-disciplined rehearsals so everyone knows what is expected down to the smallest detail.

The value of this can be emphasized and developed by stressing the results of neglect rather than those of success. While many people wish to exceed their castmates, there is an even more prevalent fear of not being able to keep up with them or of failing to make the grade.

The stereotyped performance that is caused by boredom has no remedy beyond a change in the cast during a long run, or an opportunity for promotion if the actor concerned has played the same type of role too often.

Although staleness is an enemy of inspired acting, there is much to be said in favor of the old adage about not changing horses midstream.

Some amateurs of the wrong type are inclined to give a forced impression of staleness in order to get what they imagine will be a better part. It is up to the producer and director to screen their cast for such persons and convince them they should make room for someone with the ability to cooperate.

When dealing with the small group, such as a family reunion, or the larger unrelated group, such as a crowd outside a railway station, it should be noted everyone must have something to do and their actions be logical in unity.

Remember, at all times, the view from the body of the theatre ought to resemble a pictorial composition. Harmony and balance of grouping are as important on the stage as they are on the canvas of a master painter; however, unlike the figures in an artist's picture, actors cannot stay in one place.

In order to affect a reality they have to change positions, although not too frequently, without forgoing the elements of good design.

Avoiding over-anticipation is another matter requiring careful study. This means preventing an audience from foreseeing a climax before the actual revelation.

Members of a cast often forget they see the play at an angle, rather different from the viewpoint of their audience. Thus, if actors keep turning their heads in the direction from which, let's say, a hooded Phantom is expected to make its appearance, they will either distract their audience or suggest what is likely to happen.

In both cases the character of the drama will be spoiled.

CHAPTER
eight

Rehearsals

One of the most important aspects of amateur productions concerns the way in which rehearsals are conducted. These are too frequently neglected with the big surmise that everything will be in order on the night of the play. By some miracle that may happen, but it is highly dangerous to wait for it.

The way to make rehearsals efficient is to work on a timetable. On the amateur or community level, it should be decided to hold weekly meetings on a night that is mutually convenient for all members of the cast. On the professional theatre level, it is not uncommon for rehearsals to take place daily, and during working hours. Various parts of the play can then be allotted to each rehearsal in order of a reasonable outline.

The length of time to be spent on rehearsals depends on the skill and experience of the actors, but most amateurs seem to require at least fourteen or more periods to deal with the average three-act play.

During the periods of practice, the play ought to be dealt with in simple, but definite, stages starting from scene one. On no account should there be any divergence from the original scheme, as this leads to confusion and neglect.

The various stages or periods can be worked out on call sheets, which are the blueprints for a stage production containing lists of things required at certain times and intervals.

It is necessary for all members of the cast and company to be present the first time the play is rehearsed, even though they might not appear in the parts rehearsed. In this way, they are at least learning to understand the motives and atmosphere of the production.

Before dealing with separate scenes, there should be a short discussion during which the relevant parts may be read through and outstanding questions examined.

Silence must be the rule at all rehearsals, particularly among guests and those not taking an immediate part. Conversation, however subdued, is always a distraction when there is work being done, as it distracts both those who are rehearsing and those who should be learning from rehearsals.

Learning The Parts

This may seem a rather difficult aspect of rehearsals, but practice is the only solution. The methods of learning lines may vary from group to group, but whatever these may be, the director should not be too demanding regarding accuracy of the words—that is until the last five or six rehearsals.

Try to consider and remember the actions of the play at the same time as the words. In this way, ideas are associated with deeds, which cease to be mere abstract figments of the memory.

Remembering the words with the movements is the only way in which an actor can hope to discover what is known as the texture of the play.

Dress rehearsals

These are the outstanding features of the rehearsal process. There should be at least three of them, by which time the parts should be nearly word and action perfect. This preparedness allows the director to make any vital eleventh hour changes.

Dress rehearsals are equivalent to periods for checking the results of previous work. They are not a chance to catch up on what should have been done many weeks before.

In spite of the understandable rise in spirit as the opening night approaches, discipline and calmness should be maintained at all costs. Few remember it is as easy to err through overconfidence as it is through neglect.

After the last dress rehearsal, a final word from the director on this and other matters is of great value.

Many amateurs will rehearse up to the last moment, but this is an obvious mistake, which usually hinders the progress of the final production as the cast becomes keyed up and tense through too much practice.

Good acting can never result if the characters appear to be living on their nerves, so it is an advantage to have as much restfull distraction as possible on the day of the show.

CHAPTER
nine

The Stage & Curtains

When a member of the audience is seated in the auditorium or body of the theatre, they face an archway that forms a frame around the stage. This is the proscenium arch, which is flanked by what are known as proscenium walls.

In Greek and Roman times, the proscenium was the area between the front of the stage and the rear wall of the theatre. During more recent times, it has come to be regarded as the "stage proper" or the area between the orchestra and the backcloth.

In old theatres, especially those that date to the earlier part of the 19th century, the proscenium arch was often decorated with rich moldings.

Many theatres built in modern times are of a strictly functional type. They lack the atmosphere and distinction of the old theatres and music halls, appearing almost barn-like in their simplicity.

Inside the proscenium arch you may see a secondary or false proscenium. Both arches are joined at the sides by walls known as tormentors. These were once screens or temporary walls with hinge doors; today they are sound walls of plaster and brick. The right hand tormentor as viewed from the auditorium screens the prompt corner. That is, the location where the prompter usually stands, and is also a station for the stage manager and stage assistants. The stage manager usually has a desk on the prompt side, and it is from that focal point he or she conducts a good deal of business.

Above the tormentors may be found perch lamps or raised platforms from which perch lamps are directed.

The stage is not, as many appear to think, wholly flat. Most stages are tilted or raked so that a ball would roll from the backcloth onto the footlights by means of simple gravity. If the stage were flat, the audience at the back of the auditorium would have a very poor view of the entertainment. Just as the stage slopes in one direction, the floor in many good theatres slopes at an opposite angle.

The floor of the stage may have one or more traps; these have either one or two doors seamlessly built into the stage, and cover a space or "grave" large enough to conceal a seated human figure.

Some stages are made to revolve, which is an advantage to overworked sceneshifters because the various settings can be arranged, while the play is in progress, without loss of time or strained effort.

Another type of stage is the scissor variety, which consists of two pivoted parts like the blades of a pair of scissors. The main disadvantage of both of these types is that they are ungainly and their use is not justified in a small theatre.

Curtains

Curtains may be used either to divide the front of the stage from the auditorium, or as a formal type of decor.

Front curtains are drops that can be lowered from above, and tableau curtains, or tabs, are drawn across the stage to meet each other. Tableau curtains are so called because they were formally used at the end of a play, or act, to reveal a final tableau that was to be the dramatic climax of all stage entertainment.

These early front curtains were hung in such a manner they could be drawn up into decorative scenes.

Trailers

Trailer Curtains are operated in the same manner as front tabs. They close off the back part of the stage, about four or five feet from the footlights, while the set is being changed. This allows a short scene to be acted in front of them, while a more elaborate setting is prepared behind. Thus long periods of waiting are avoided, which is a great advantage in a play with many scenes. Trailers are usually lighter in weight, material and color compared to the main tabs and other curtains.

Pelmets

Pelmet Curtains serve as a border, and are often cut from elaborate material or heavily braided. The intent is to frame the top of the stage and conceal the running tracks on which other curtains are moved.

Deep helmets are also used to decrease the height of the stage when the effect is thought necessary.

Leg Curtains

The Leg Curtains are often used in place of more elaborate flats or sections of scenery. They are either fixed to hinge frames, which may be folded into a small area, or hung from a grid frame above the stage. When they are hung it should be noted the frame or grid covers the stage area and has rods or battens which are suspended crosswise at various intervals.

The best means of hanging leg curtains from the battens is to attach a length of braid to which rings may be sewn along the top of one side. If they are sewn any nearer to the top the audience will see them, even when the ringed side is reversed. The rings should fit on hooks that are screwed into the wood.

Color leg curtains and trailers should be in pastel shades. The main tabs and drops must be an outstanding color, leaning on the cool side. Thus, if red is chosen, it should be crimson rather than scarlet. This contrast of effects makes the curtains seem more impressive.

Curtain Tracks

The types of tracks sold for hanging ordinary window curtains are not strong enough to bear the weight of main tabs. They may be strong enough for light trailers, but even for these they are unsuitable as they are apt to jam and stick at the wrong moment.

Although some amateurs make their own curtain tracks, these are rarely efficient and often spoil the atmosphere by making a strange clattering noise.

The only satisfactory solution is to buy special equipment that is effective and soundless. Tracks may be bought in a variety of lengths and are often doubled so the reverse side of the curtains can be shown to full advantage.

CHAPTER
ten

Scenery

The use of scenery in the theatre is a more recent development. The Greeks, Romans and miracle players of the Middle Ages preferred to act in front of a plain background or conventional set., i.e. something with limited architectural features. It was not until the Renaissance that the illusion of realistic architecture on landscape was introduced.

In modern times, there are several important trends. Most of these first became popular between 1920 and 1938, although many of them are rarely seen in the ordinary theatre. The most outstanding are constructionism and naturalism, which have decorative and symbolic offshoots. Naturalism or realism aims at reproducing nature in a forward manner, while constructionism reduces both decoration and the sense of reality to bare essentials.

Constructionism is the main doctrine applied to the stage. Instead of furniture and artificial trees the audience must be content with other things and projections exposed without ornament or relief.

The scene which has been made according to these ideals is easy enough to construct, but must be carefully designed by an expert who understands modern art. For this reason, amateurs should confine themselves to naturalism; with realistic stage design, interiors are the most elaborate and difficult to handle.

Not only does the furniture need to be arranged to make a pleasing effect by avoiding obvious parallels and giving the actors enough room, but the designer also meets with the problem of walls, doors, windows and even fireplaces.

The conventional stage interior is usually known as a box set, as it is made in the form of a three-sided box with an imaginary fourth wall and roof. Each wall is made of hinged or unhinged, but connected, sections known as flats. These are made of wood and canvas, and are usually about twelve feet high. They are braced at the back with iron rods that are weighted or screwed onto the stage.

In fact, each flat is often used as a ground or agent for the scene painter. Special scenic canvas is available for the purpose of making flats and other parts of scenery, and this ought to be used in the place of inferior substitutes that will not take the paint and eventually result in sagging.

Doors and windows are openings constructed in the flats with moldings and ledges built up out of wooden strips. Panels on doors should be constructed, rather than painted on flat surfaces, and picture-rail molding is ideal for this purpose. All doors should be made of wood, the thicker the better, so they do not appear to bend and wobble when moved. At one time, canvas doors were used—these brought on unseemly laughter when disturbed by a slight current of air.

All well-constructed stage windows and doors should have an outer framework or casing to make them appear to fit into the masonry. In constructing doors, see that they open inwardly as much as possible. It would be unusual for a window to open in this way, but when interior doors are used these should open onto the set. A door that opens outward and off the stage will usually cast a shadow in the wrong place and makes the area offstage seem shallow and unconvincing.

A piece of scenery known as a baking flat is placed behind the doors and windows in order to counteract this impression and create the idea of a mental view of events.

In dealing with period interiors, the problem of correct furnishing is more difficult than that of a modern set. If authentic looking furniture cannot be hired or borrowed, improvisations or the plainest modern furniture should be used in its place. This does not mean tubular steel chairs and glass top tables, which are favored in some advanced circles, but ordinary kitchen furniture of simple design.

When providing an interior setting with pictures, vases and other ornaments, they should be bright and colorful, but in good taste. There is a tendency among some to consider these points of decor as unimportant, but this is a serious mistake.

Members of the audience with good taste and commonsense are apt to be annoyed by the presence of poorly chosen ornaments, and this will reflect on the whole production.

However, it must be remembered that some interiors require definite vulgarity just as some human characters need grotesque makeup. This factor should be taken into account when the room is designed so that whatever the result, it is never haphazard or ill planned.

When designing a set, local atmosphere is an important matter to be taken into account. In this respect, the audience will expect to find framed sporting prints in the room of a country inn, and maps on the walls of the school room. Very few audiences will tolerate the effect of confusing different types of motif.

Artists and Painters

It is always useful to have one or two painters attached to a group. These skilled creatives can help in the design and production of setting, and may also give advice concerning costume, publicity and other matters, which are akin to artistic matters.

CHAPTER
eleven

Stage Lighting

Lighting is one of the purely technical matters connected with the stage for which one requires the help and advice of a specialist. These notes are not set down in an attempt to teach the expert his business, but as a general guide to an electrician who is without knowledge of theatre practice.

There are two main kinds of lighting, which are known either as floods or spots. The floods dispense light over a general area, while the spots are concentrated on a particular part of the stage.

Floodlighting is used in rows for footlights and border lights, or as separate units in places where extra brilliance is required. The earlier method of footlighting, which consisted of placing separate electric lamps a few inches apart, is now thought wasteful and inadequate. Footlights today are often built into a form of a trough that can be lowered and hidden beneath the stage. This means there will always be a slight projection of the footlights above stage level, but this need not be considered a serious obstruction.

Spotlights are now considered among the most valuable and important assets of the modern stage. Most up-to-date stages have at least a dozen spots, but their numbers may vary according to the size and importance of the theatre to well over a hundred.

Spot Positioning

Bar spots are hung from horizontal tubes that are wired internally. These may be suspended above the number one batten, which extends across the stage near the inside of the false proscenium arch.

Perch spots are found between the proscenium arch and the false proscenium arch, and are sometimes fixed to the walls.

Wing spots shine onto the stage from the wings. These are fitted to the wall brackets known as "boomerangs." However, they may be fitted to movable standards mounted on wheels or casters.

Front spots, or front of the house spots, are erected in the auditorium. They may be attached to the front of the balcony or any supporting columns in the theatre. They are usually operated by remote control, but are sometimes operated and directed by hand.

Mirror spots are an elaborate type of lamp, shedding a strong, narrow beam for special effects. These are also considered front spots.

Switchboard

The switchboard is specified as the switch-and-dimmer board, and may be called, in theatrical jargon, the stage board.

Variations of the stage board include three important types, of which the most outstanding is the slider dimmer. This has two coils of resistance wire with a contact that slides between them. The slider dimmer is cheap to buy and simple to operate, but can be used with no more than twelve dimmers.

If more than this number is required, portable dimmer boards, which interlock with the original system, are available. There is also a type of dimmer that has a hundred steps or stages for various intensities of lighting. The brush, fixed to a movable arm, maintains the contact being worked over the studs or steps.

The dimmers have handles, and these can be screwed onto a shaft and operated by turning a capstan wheel. This allows the operator to employ a broad simultaneous effect. A thorough and well-trained person should carry out all of this insulation.

Careless workmanship in this department may lead to serious accidents in the worst-case scenarios, and inefficiency at the best.

When fitting the stage with lighting, the best possible material should be bought. As good stage lighting often counteracts deficiencies of scenery and costume, by a small token, the best decor is ruined by poor illumination.

CHAPTER
twelve

Sound Effects

This chapter is designed to give you a brief overview of how sound equipment has worked. Since technology is always evolving, many of these methods have changed—and will continue to change in the future. For example, many theatres now have the capabilities to use 100 percent digital sound recordings, with an endless supply of sounds. That, combined with the use of live orchestra effects, makes up a lot of tech that goes into sound during modern day.

Sound effects may be classified under three different headings, as follows:

A. Sound effects recorded on a machine.

B. Sound effects made with the voice, hands or feet.

C. Sounds made by machinery other than recorders or recordings.

Category A

In the first category, sound effects are recorded on a machine, and offer a limited range of conventional sounds, such as birds singing, a ship's horn or vehicular traffic.

Sound or stage effects records may vary in having from three to eight different sets of noises on each or both sides; however, as a general rule, each type of record is limited to particular kinds of effects.

Thus, if the title of the record was "In a Barnyard" the mooing of the cattle, the crowing of a rooster and the grinding of cartwheels might be expected. The sounds on records are divided from each other by blank

48

spaces on the surface of the recording, and have, in most cases, the disadvantage of short duration.

Prolonged noises should be made by other methods, as repetitions of the same record are not only halting but also easily recognized, which makes them seem artificial.

Types of record players vary from the large cabinet models to portable machines about the size of an attaché case or smaller. The speed, and revolutions per minute, is indicated on the label of each record. The best effect is obtained by keeping the lid of the machine closed. Records should not be left about in odd places, as they are easily chipped and broken and expensive to replace. They should be kept in special record albums or stored between layers of cardboard and paper. It is also better to lay them flat rather than to stand them on end, as the former method of storage preserves the edges from damage. Finally, all dust and grit must be removed from the surface of records before and after use. It is also necessary to keep dust from accumulating on or near the vital parts of the recorder.

Category B

In the second category, sound effects made with the voice, hands or feet, limitations are those of talent rather than expenditure or space. Some groups are fortunate enough to have members who are gifted mimics. Such people may be able to produce all kinds of vocal sounds, representing anything from a bird to motorcycle. When that kind of talent is not available, many improvisations can be made with cheap material.

For example, train noises can be done by working a roller skate with the hand on a sheet of lead that has been nailed to the top of a strong box. Noises such as doors being slammed are simulated by stamping on a wooden floorboard or by kicking the box. Several people hissing between their front teeth can make the noise of escaping steam, which might occur when the train arrives at a station.

There is a popular tradition that hoof beats must be made with parts of a coconut shell; however, a couple of plastic beakers are just as good, if not better. If, when using beakers, the noise sounds rather high pitched this can be lowered by lining the outside of each vessel with rags.

Ship sirens and foghorns can be simulated by blowing and groaning through a megaphone.

The effect of a window or china smashing is produced by pouring fragments of broken glass or china out of a small cardboard box onto a tray of wood or metal.

Explosions are made either by simple percussion, such as beating a drum or gong, or by firing a blank cartridge gun into a large metal tank.

Wherever possible, actual noises in the nature of closing windows and slamming doors should be made on stage in the normal course of events.

Category C

Effects machines are the third category, and the mechanisms are either constructed for the stage or improvised from existing equipment, such as a lawnmower or carpet sweepers.

Recognized apparatuses include the rain box, thunder cart and wind machine. The rain box usually consists of a long box or tube pierced on the inside by long nails that penetrate the interior. The box is mounted on a pivoted stand so that it may revolve or move up or down, according to your handling it. When the instrument is ready for use, it is partly filled with dried peas, which rattle against the nails with every movement of the box.

The thunder cart is a small but heavy vehicle with solid wheels that make a noise like a roll of thunder when it is weighted and dragged over a hard surface. Making the wheels bent and uneven increases the volume of the sound. In most theatres, the thunder cart has been replaced. They use what is called a thunder sheet, which is a sizable though convenient strip of sheet metal, suspended from a strong wooden beam. This is struck with a blunt instrument in the same matter as a gong to produce a variety of tones.

A wind machine is a hand operated drum supported by a strong bar, like an old-fashioned butter churn. Raised strips of wood are attached to the circumference of the drum at equally spaced intervals. A sheet of canvas is then secured to a weight or crossbar below the drum and the free end of the cloth is laid over the top of the drum and weighted on the opposite side. When the drum is turned by means of a handle fitted to the axle, the raised strips grind against the canvas and make tearing sounds like a high wind.

Hand operated machines are found to be the most suitable and effective for producing stage noises, as power driven inventions are rarely full proof and reliable. While the hand machine that breaks down can be repaired in a few minutes it's counterpart may need extensive replacements and lengthy overhauls.

CHAPTER
thirteen

Costumes

The importance of costume is a debatable point. Many people are so interested in this aspect of the production they get great pleasure from admiring the clothes worn by the actors and actresses. Others are usually blasé to a point of indifference; they fail to notice mistakes in costumes and are even content to see Shakespeare acted in modern dress.

As a rule, the less serious and austere the quality of entertainment, the more interests the general audience is inclined to take in the costumes. The high standard of costume design in musical productions such as "Annie Get Your Gun," "Kiss Me Kate" and "South Pacific" tends to prove this statement.

Here are some hints for dressing a cast.

On the whole, it is much better to rent the costumes than to attempt to make them, unless you have a well-staffed and skillful costume team.

If renting is impossible, and you do not have a team to create costumes, ordinary clothes for which the owner has no further use can be adapted. Typically, amateurs take that path. For this reason, it is advisable to have a good dressmaker or needlewoman in the wardrobe department.

For male roles, light overcoats and pants can be cut down and altered to form dress coats and knickers.

Colors and materials for costumes

Great care has to be taken in choosing the right colors to agree with dramatic and lighting effects. There can be no hard and fast rules in this respect, but it is generally considered certain colors and materials are safer and more dependable than others. This is because the strength and intensity of stage lighting has a bleaching influence while exaggerating the texture as well.

Velvet is a difficult type of material to use, as it has a peculiar sheen, and in some lights is robbed of its color and form. Even the darker velvets tend to lose their richness and become drab. Silks, satins and most types of cotton and woolen fabrics are fairly safe, but experiments ought to be made in each case before the dress rehearsals.

Regardless, one cardinal rule must be observed. You have to dress your actors and actresses according to the particular time period involved with each play you produce.

For example, if it were the 1920s, it would look ridiculous to dress the cast in today's modern attire. My advice for amateurs setting up a new theatre is to have a good wardrobe and costume department. Having that is as much of a key to having a good director, actors and all aspects involved with your shows.

CHAPTER
fourteen

Makeup

The art of makeup and drama have developed together through the ages. Early cave dwellers, in common with aborigines of Australia and Africa, covered their faces and bodies with grease and colored clay before taking part in tribal rituals.

In the Far East, it has long been a tradition for actors to stain their faces with grotesque dyes, with different colors being reserved for certain character parts.

Modern grease paint was introduced in 1873, several years before the use of electric lighting in theatres. Until this time, makeup was crude and garish. Yet, although the introduction of grease paint caused changes, the revolution in stage lighting during the second half of the century was also responsible for general improvement.

The standard grease paint can be obtained in a large variety of colors, including several flesh tints. These may be used to create the illusion of youthful freshness or of wrinkled old age, but it should be remembered that incorrect or excessive application is not advised in most cases.

The right type of grease paint should be tacky enough to hold the powder applied over its foundation. In addition to ordinary grease paints, other requisites include liners, rouges, removing cream, eyebrow and lip pencils, eye shadow, tooth enamel and nose putty. Also, liquid makeup for the body is something many actors use.

Liners

These are forms of grease paint, but are made in much narrower sticks than those used for foundation purposes. They are mainly used for the imitation or emphasis of natural lines on the face and neck. Liner can also be used in shading and blending whenever fine shading is required.

Rouges and Powders

These are used in the final stages of complete makeup. They are applied over the grease paint and cream rouge, or without the former, to exemplify dry makeup. However, the latter should be used as a temporary method that is not recommended in general practice.

Eyebrow and Lip Pencils

These are used to accentuate or increase the natural contours of the eyebrows and mouth.

Eye Shadows

These are cosmetics for treating the eyelids. There are several ranges of color, from blue to green and mauve. They should not be confused with eyelash darkening cosmetics and mascara, which are used to intensify the color and curl of the lashes.

Tooth Enamel

This can be used in a dark tint to blackout teeth, or light to correct dullness. It is harmless to use, and can be easily removed with a small quantity of liquid on a soft rag.

Nose Putty

Nose putty is used for modeling outstanding parts of features. Despite the name, it can be applied to any external part of the body. The putty should always be warmed and kneaded before use, and disguised beneath a normal layer of makeup.

Corrective Makeup

The art of corrective makeup is used to improve natural defects of face and features. It is widely practiced, as few people are without some small defect. Increasing the contours of the lips with the proper pencil normally enlarges the appearance of the mouth. Making the mouth smaller appears to increase the size of the face. When eyes are deeply set in the sockets very little eye shadow should be used. If the eyes are too prominent, the eye shadow must be increased.

Wigs

A wig should never be worn if there is plausible opportunity for appearing with natural hair. This is typically determined by the theatre, and in some or most cases with large professional theatres undertaking eight to ten shows per week; there is a lot of wig use to protect the actors' natural hair.

Skillful though their creation maybe, they always have an appearance of ruffled perfection that makes them look artificial. Yet, in spite of all of this, certain period character parts cannot be played without a transformation. Make sure when obtaining a wig that it suits the character of the wearer's role, and that it is a good fit.

CHAPTER
fifteen

The Program & Publicity

L ocal stationers and printers are often established in even the smallest country towns, and they're fit to deal with program and publicity printing.

With most playbills and other visual aids to publicity, unusual lettering should be avoided. Insist on a good lettering and stay away from flamboyant or ornamental fonts that some printers think essential for any form of entertainment literature. It is a wise plan to draw up a simple sketch or a layout of the way in which the lettering is to be distributed on the paper and submit this to the printer and designer before any printing is done.

Many programs consist of more than a single page, and there should be a design or pictorial motif depicting the show theme. As well, the title of the play and the name of the performing company should appear boldly.

Remember to give full credit to all of the performers and assistants, and make special mention of anyone who has been kind enough to lend properties such as furniture.

Do not make the author's name inconspicuous, as this will seem an insult to one who is quite as important as members of the cast. If advertisements are included in the program, which is a good idea to build funds as they may help to cover production costs, see that there are not too many of them and that they harmonize with the general scheme of lettering and layout.

Publicity

There is no point in offering anything to the public if people are not made aware of its existence. The bridge between producer and consumer, or audience and performer, is publicity. This can be as important to the success of the show as the design, stage settings or the choice of production itself.

Playbills are one of the main means of theatrical publicity. If however the play is to include the appearance of a well-known actor or actress, it will be an advantage to put out the playbills earlier.

A useful aid to theatrical publicity is a shop window display in a busy part of the nearest town or shopping center. This may include photographs of the actors taken in normal grouping, or tableau at dress rehearsals. The distribution of hand bills either in the streets or from door to door should be discouraged, as it makes litter and irritates householders. A loudspeaker van is more of a nuisance than advantage.

Finally, I highly suggest you contact any local papers and enlist the services of their theatrical reviewers. Have these critics review your show, either at a dress rehearsal or on opening night. Instruct them so they have the history of the show posted at the top of their article. In addition to a list that includes all details regarding the show, such as dates of the run, cost of a ticket, box office number and location of the theatre. Try to get a paper locally that will not only run your review of the production in their papers but will list online as well.

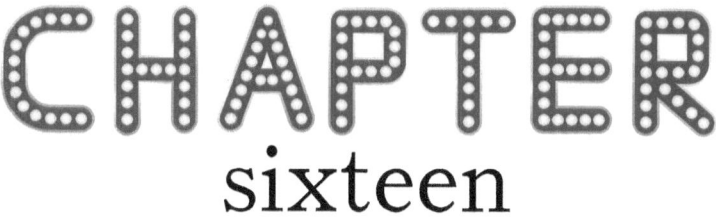

sixteen

Drama

To all beginners that have stayed with me as we covered all aspects of theatre, now permit me to invite you to continue the journey as I define in more depth as to what theatre is all about.

Dra-Ma (Dra'ma - Dram'a)

Definition A:
A prose or verse composition, especially one telling a serious story that is intended for representation by actors impersonating the characters and performing the dialogue and action.
Definition B:
A serious narrative work or program for television, radio or the movies.

There are many different forms of drama; the following will give you more meaning as to what drama is all about.

Catharsis: (in the Aristotelian concept of art, especially with reference to tragic drama) the purging of the emotions, traditionally said to be those of pity and fear.

Choreodrama: a drama expressed in dance or with dance as an integral part of its content and form.

Denouncement: The final resolution of the plot, following the climax.

Deuteragonist: Greek drama, the role that is second in importance to that of the protagonist, or main character.

Dramalogue: A dramatic monologue.

Dramaturgy: The art of writing or producing plays.

Duodrama: A play or drama for two characters or actors.

Duologue: A dialogue for two people, especially as a complete dramatic performance or as part of one.

Epilogue: The final section of a literary work, often added by way of explanation, comments, etc., or a closing speech in a play often delivered after the completion of the main action.

Epitasis: The main action of the drama, leading up to the catastrophe.

Exode: Greek drama, the catastrophe or conclusion of the play; or Roman drama, a comical or satirical piece added at the end of the play.

Melodrama: A sensational drama with events and emotions extravagantly expressed, or an opera or stage play with songs and music, often of a romantic nature.

Monodrama: A drama written for one actor or character.

Classical Drama: The first part of a play, when the characters are introduced.

Soliloquy: A speech in which a character reveals their thoughts to the audience, but not to other characters in the play.

Theatrics: the art of the theatre or of acting.

Theatromania: A mania or love for the theatre.

Drama is the specific mode of fiction represented in performance. The term comes from a Greek word meaning "action," which is derived from the verb meaning "to do" or "to act." The enactment of drama in theatre, performed by actors on a stage before an audience, presupposes collaborative mode of production and collective forms of literature.

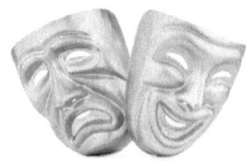

The two masks associated with drama represent the traditional division between comedy and tragedy. They are symbols of the ancient Greek muses, Thalia and Melpomene. Thalia was the muse of comedy (the laughing face), while Melpomene was the muse of tragedy (the weeping face).

Drama is often combined with music and dance. The drama in Opera is generally sung throughout, musicals mainly include both spoken dialogue and songs and some forms of drama have incidental music or musical accompaniment underscoring the dialogue—such as melodrama and Japanese Noh, for example.

In certain periods of history, for example, the ancient Roman and modern romantic, some dramas were written to be read rather than performed.

CHAPTER
seventeen

Comedy & Improvisation

Comedy

In the contemporary meaning of the term, comedy is any discourse or work generally intended to be humorous or to amuse by inducing laughter.

Satire and political satire use ironic comedy to portray persons or social institutions as ridiculous or corrupt.

Screwball comedy derives its humor largely from bizarre, surprising (and improbable) situations or characters.

Black or dark comedy is defined by dark humor that makes light of so-called dark or evil elements and human nature. Similarly, harsh humor, sexual humor and race humor create comedy by violating social conventions or taboos in comic ways.

A comedy of manners typically takes as its subject a particular part of society (usually upper class society) and uses humor to parody or satirize the behavior and mannerisms of its members.

Romantic comedy is a popular genre that depicts burgeoning romance and humorous terms while focused on the stories of those who are falling in love.

Let's review a little background on the origins of comedy.

Ancient Greeks and Romans confined the word "comedy" to descriptions of stage plays with happy endings. In the Middle Ages, the term expanded to include narrative poems with happy endings and a lighter tone. As time progressed, the word came more and more to be associated with any sort of performance intended to cause laughter.

There are many words that define the term comedy, such as humor, fun, joking, farce, jesting, slapstick, wisecracking, hilarity, witticisms and facetiousness.

Remember, although drama requires constant concentration of your feelings and those of other actors around you, comedy is based strictly on timing—knowing when to make certain movements either facial or body. It's crucial to intersect your remarks properly as the situation dictates.

Two of the greatest comics of another era Jack Benny and Red Skelton are perfect examples of this. Jack Benny could simply stand still, reacting only facially, or by putting one hand under one of his elbows as a result of someone's remarks, or if he was telling a supposedly true story.

The audience would be wrapped in laughter.

Red Skelton, playing a buffoon or the poor soul, with basic simple movements created outrageous humor.

There is one other that comes to mind; Sid Caesar, with his ability to use dialects and proper movements, was outstanding.

Sir Philip Sydney who wrote "The Difference of Poetry," once said, "Comedy is an imitation of the common errors of our life."

That said, another form of comedy or drama is improvisation, which is defined: to compose and perform without preparation. To make or do whatever is at hand.

With this comedic style you don't go for jokes, you simply improvise.

An example is having a discussion with another person telling them about your day's adventures and how it transpired into ridiculous happenings. Or, stories of your life growing up as the only boy, or girl, with three sisters or three brothers would be another fine example of using improvisation skills.

It is considered one of the simplest and easiest forms of humor you can do. You can also use improvisation in creating an incident of drama you experienced. Many in an audience will relate to what you are saying, as it will remind them of similar events they themselves experienced.

Remember in improvisation:
1. There are no bad ideas.
2. There are no mistakes.
3. Everything is justified.
4. Keep it simple.
5. Take the scene seriously.

CHAPTER
eighteen

Auditions

One of the most important events (and possibly traumatic experiences) in an actor or actress' career, whether they be an amateur, beginner or for that matter experienced, is called the audition!

Most theatres post notices of upcoming auditions for roles in their upcoming productions via online methods, or some within their theatres or even by word-of-mouth.

In general, all theatres usually announce if it is an open audition, but that's not always true. Some have definite people they favor for the role. It is up to you to have the mentality and desire to do your very best to convince the decision-makers, which often consist of the director, assistant director, producers, play reading chairperson, casting and artistic director and maybe even the music director if it's a musical.

In their posting, theatres will often provide the story of the show. In addition to roles and descriptions, if it's a non-musical they ask you to do a short monologue, and cold readings of the script.

With a musical, they will have you sing a prepared song and cold readings.

I suggest anyone going to an audition visit a library or search online to secure a script, storyline, character descriptions and historical background for the role and play he or she is striving to take part. Gathering this information will help you decide what other role or roles you might be interested in, and capable of doing.

By the way, if it is a musical, try to locate or rent a recording of the music itself. Listening to it will help you hear the range of the music the show entails.

Some shows or roles may entail a background in an area different from where you grew up. So, if you have the ability to change your voice or even body language, it could it be an advantage in your favor.

At the audition, if you give a monologue, try to select a monologue relative to the type of show you are auditioning for. If it is a drama, select something dramatic; if a comedy, something comedic. The same method applies to singing for musicals; pick a song relative to the show.

Audition Tips

1. Read the script many times prior to the audition so you are familiar with the show.
2. You can memorize some lines; however, if a theatre doesn't post what parts will be read it could backfire on you. Be prepared for your planning to be altered if that occurs.
3. If a dialect is required, and you can perform it well, always ask the director first if you should read it straight or with a dialect.
4. Try to move as you read the script, but only as it pertains to the character you are performing. Interact with other potential actors or actresses reading with you.
5. Always be polite.
6. Never try to come across as a know-it-all.
7. At the end, thank everyone who is concerned with judging your audition. Let them know you would enjoy doing this role.

So you made it through the audition and now you got the part! Next, you are scheduled to meet up with your fellow cast for a read-through of the script. Congrats!

Read as you did at the auditions. Keep your character in mind at all times when at the read-through, or any rehearsals, as you take on the mantle of the role you will portray.

CHAPTER
nineteen

How to Relate to a Director

The definition of an actor is one who represents fictitious or historical characters in the play, simply one who acts.

The definition of a director is the manager of the interactive aspects of the stage production who supervises such elements as the acting.

Although we are all actors every day on the big stage of life, remember an actor is an extension of the director.

Allow me to elaborate...

In order for an actor to succeed, there has to be a proper understanding between the actor and the director.

It's very important the actor is open with the director and understands what the director is trying to get out of the role. If an actor is concerned about their performance, blocking or characterization, they should always discuss this with the director.

These conversations should take place during dedicated note times, or off to the side, but never in front of the entire cast.

Never go to fellow actors for their opinion on your concerns, or let another actor tell you what to do. Politely decline their offer to help you and talk to your director. Most good directors would be willing to try something in a way you suggest. If it doesn't look right to them, then you have to rely on the director's experience.

By discussing things with your director, it forms a better working relationship and mutual respect is established. This does not mean you should question every direction or character development and movement, as this could cause chaos and dissension among all involved.

Remember there is only one director, and your job as an actor is to act.

Finally, there is one way a director can better relate to his cast. He or she should always treat everyone with respect—whether they get paid or not, are on a professional level or a community theatre level.

If a director notices something wrong, he or she should always talk to the person, group or tech people concerned, not in front of the entire cast but off to the side.

You will always get more out of your cast with respect. No one actor or tech person deserves to be screamed at and embarrassed. You will most likely be rewarded with a happy, respected and respectful cast and tech crew for doing this.

I will deal with this in more detail in another chapter.

CHAPTER
twenty

Memorization & Breaking Down a Script

The American College Dictionary defines the word memorize as "to commit to memory or to learn by heart."

There are many ways to learn to memorize. For example, if you were trying to remember many names, you can say the name constantly in addressing them or equate them to something that sounds the same i.e. you could imagine Mr. Brown wearing a brown suit.

As far as learning lines for a role, I suggest the following basic order:

1. Understand who and what your character is all about. This way lines will come easier as the character you are portraying is fully understood by you.

2. Read the script many times before you undertake memorizing the lines. This will help you understand the storyline and your character's contribution to the play. A director will help you mold your character.

3. Now you are ready to begin. Underline or highlight all of your lines with a light yellow or light green highlighter so they are easy to recognize and read.

4. Break down each act and scene by numbering the pages of your dialogue. For example, if you have five lines on a page that counts as one page of dialogue. Example: Act I, scene one, five pages, and scenes two through eight pages. Act

II, one through ten pages, scene two through seven pages. That results in a total of thirty pages of dialogue.

5. Then, according to the amount of rehearsal time, learn two or three pages per day. Always repeat them out loud to yourself. If possible, it is especially helpful to have someone hold the script until you feel confident. The next day, repeat them and take on the next set of pages. Another way is to make a recording of your lines and enlist someone to do the other characters' lines. Cast your husband, wife or a good friend in these roles of helpful assistants.

6. Learning lines is basically repetition so repeat, repeat and repeat.

7. To help yourself, other cast members and particularly the director, when you get the script well in advance, start the memorization process immediately. That way, when the director starts blocking you will feel more comfortable.

8. The way you use your character, voice and movement will help trigger your memory. So, be sure you are thinking about your character's important traits well ahead of your memorization, and as you go through the memorization process.

There are two cardinal rules that you as an actor should always keep in mind.

1. Be prepared to bail out a fellow actor who might go blank on stage, by continuing the dialogue relevance to the storyline and scene. Once they come back to reality, just hit them with their cue lines. The audience will never notice as long as activity keeps going.

2. By accepting a role, large or small, it is your commitment to learn your lines.

Many actors can learn lines and don't take it further, but to become a true performer you must take on the mantle of the character. The most boring thing for an audience is to hear someone just saying lines. Character requires body language, facial expression and proper inflection of your voice.

Finally, you have to project your voice; don't swallow your words or sentences. You can't always depend on body microphones as they may break down on occasion.

Note: The following chapters will deal with different areas of the theatre venue itself and its organization.

CHAPTER
twenty-one

The Stage as a World

Toward the close of the 16th century, the theatre, which had set its stage in amphitheaters, cathedrals, marketplaces and courtyards, crowded itself indoors, its stage constricted between an ornate frame—the proscenium—and a blank wall.

This space became shallower with every succeeding generation as the concentration of populations into cities raised the cost of building sites.

At the beginning of the 19th century, the world pictured in the theatre had become a world of paint and canvas as flat and shallow as the stage it occupied.

In 1890, Antoine exclaimed, "We are still using ridiculous backdrops which have no atmosphere or depth, on which we do not hesitate to paint furniture or even a staircase within three feet of the footlights."

Any interior seemed an enlarged dollhouse. Every exterior had an air of having been cut out of cardboard, set up as a plaything of a titanic child would have been.

The canvas tree trunks of a forest faced each other in parallel rows; above them hung parallel layers of serrated canvas for foliage. At the beginning of the 20th century, a certain number of modern painters entered the theatre, first in Germany and Russia, then in Austria, France and England, and finally reaching the United States.

With the aid of the electrician, they created behind the proscenium frame, some of the beauty you see today.

During the past century, pictorial beauty in the theatre has become a new tradition and the technique of achieving it part of the technique of play producing itself.

Another Fine Art

Although its materials are intrinsically tawdry and its forms fugitive, the designing of stage settings in the United States has, within the past so some odd years, been added to the roster of fine arts, a place accorded previously to scenic design in Europe.

The American scene designer was, as a rule, a scene painter—an anonymous craftsman turning out stock patterns or stereotyped backdrops by the square yard and delivering them to the stage door without much interest as to their effect in the theatre.

Today, the role adopts the pretensions and accepts the responsibilities of any other artist.

Not only do audiences applaud the work at the rise of the curtain, but the designer is also held accountable by the director and actors for his or her share in the interpretation of the script. The role is accepted as a definite part of any performance. If successful work is achieved for the show, the designer's scrapbook will bulge with clippings and notices like any leading actor.

Sin and Salutation

For slightly more than seventy-five years, the effort to define the original sin of theatrical art, and the attempt to establish an orthodox method for the theatre's salutation has persisted.

Drama was to become a succession of mystic revelations mimed by mechanical puppets that were to have the dignity and grace of a set of gods.

It was solemnly predicted that when this new art of the theatre had been perfected, it would be so divine a new religion would be founded upon it. No one succeeded in articulating the super marionette. Thankfully, actors continued to gesticulate and to use their vocal chords.

Holiday

The unmistakable brilliance of such recent visions of a new theatre is due to the fact that, like searchlights prodding the night, their focus is only large enough to isolate a single object. In the enveloping darkness the structure of society of which the theatre is a part can be found.

Today, the relation of the modern theatre to its audience is not much different from what it was when tragedy and comedy were supposedly born on an attic hillside.

The form of any theatre is determined not by the kind of dramatic literature it expects to house, for that can never be foreseen, but by the holiday habits of its people. These are determined, in turn, by an entire connection of social, political, religious and economic habits, customs and taboos that have no relation to the theatre whatsoever.

We in the Western world have always gone to the theatre as part of a holiday—a week, a day, an afternoon or evening off. From our cubicles in apartment houses and hotels, as well as our individual homes, to the blinking electric lights of Broadway we head. Our destination? All community, repertory and professional dinner theatres in the outlying areas of where we live.

We can stand at any theatre door as Faust did at the city's gate and see a populous release, escape...

"Out of the musty cells of humble homes, out of the bonds of trade and handicrafts, out of the crushing straightness of the streets, and exclaim with him, 'here is the people's heaven.' "

We go not only to see a show, but also to be part of the show ourselves. To show off in our best clothes, our finery, our jewels if we have any.

We go to feel our contact with the great world under a single roof, within the circle of a single arena or the boundaries of a single public square; to see the guardians of the state at the edge of the stage.

A play can be rehearsed to a handful of spectators, but what theatre has ever aimed to perform its plays except to the crowds?

We go to the theatre to be part of the crowd, to experience an electric extension of our personality, to laugh with a thousand throats, to roar approval with a thousand voices and to clap with two thousand hands. We become part of a mass that has power, one that is, for an hour or two, passing irrevocable judgment, conferring favor and success, decreeing failure and oblivion.

The elemental satisfaction in theatre-going for every playgoer from pit to gallery, from the first ring of an amphitheater to its top-most retaining wall, is this overwhelming release of emotion and the sense of power its expression gives one in contact with the crowd of his fellows.

A theatre then is a holiday center to hold a vociferous crowd, eager not only to laugh and weep, but also to applaud, stamp, hiss, cheer.

It has always been built for that purpose with rule-of-thumb expediency.

A play occurs first of all when it is written. It is acted in the mind of the playwright before it is acted in front of an audience. Before it is performed in the theatre, it has already taken place.

Dr. Jones' drawing room is Dr. Jones' drawing room, whether the moldings of its doors and windows are subsequently imitated on the stage with painted canvas or with solid wood.

The dramatist of imagination does not write for any particular theatre. The theatre approximates his word as best it can. The playwrights everywhere, at all times, give their imagination free reign; pictures and spectacles have always been an inherent part of their imaginings.

Throughout the entire history of the theatre, the constant job of the stage technician, like that of the actor, has been to keep at the heels of dramatic poets. For those poets, whose imaginations make everything possible, sooner or later have creativity catch up with them, and the playwrights' worlds on the stage become as real to an audience as to the playwright.

Stagecraft, at best, is nothing more than the tail to the poet's kite. Designers and mechanics hold the string so that the kite can soar.

In so far as the playwright is an artist, they not only portray deeds but also penetrate to the meaning of motive and emotion that breeds them and gives them understanding. They express a fresh sense of the springs of human character and the values of human experience.

He or she learns this outside the theatre, not within it.

The dull and lifeless epochs of playwriting are invariably those when dramatists see life too nearly in terms of the theatre and repeat some one method of fitting the pattern of life into the frame of a particular stage.

The theatre comes to life at intervals when a dramatist such as Euripides, Shakespeare, Molière, Ibsen, Shaw or O'Neill sees life in the theatre in terms of what he believes to be the truth of life about him.

We have accepted, as the best description of the playwrights' vision, the assertion: all the world is a stage. But to the playwright, as they write, any stage is all the world.

CHAPTER
twenty-two

Realism & Reality

<u>Mind's Eye</u>

Dramatic geniuses that revolutionized the methods of writing plays rarely make a single innovation in the method of staging them. A performance is, at best, an inadequate approximation of an event that has already taken place in the limitless realm of the imagination.

Like the most uninspired journeyman, the dramatist wants to get his play put on, and, in order to have it acted, will accept any convention that the theatre of his day imposes.

A great play lives in its day, as third-rate ones do, by its ability to touch the passions, prejudices, ideals, ambitions, hopes and memories of its generation. The actors' dominance depends not upon any physical relation to his spectators, but upon his power to stir the imagination.

The reality of a theatrical performance has no inherit connection with its realism, the degree of fidelity with which it reproduces or reflects the facts, as we say, of actual life. A play becomes real to the degree that any audience succeeds in identifying itself with the lives and deeds portrayed.

Events on a stage are real to us because we accept them as true although they occur, supposedly, in heaven or hell. A dramatic story becomes unreal the moment it fails to convince us it is a true account of human nature and human motives, even if it takes place in a wonderful reproduction of a tenement-house kitchen.

No amount of imitation of nature, such as water running through the faucets into the kitchen sink, or gas whistling in the kitchen stove, can make the play an imitation of life if we find it to be false to what we conceive "real life" to be.

Once we accept the play and say to ourselves, "This is the way things happen, this is real, this is true," our conviction can be reinforced by natural detail. However, it cannot be created or destroyed because faucets, with great artistic restraint, fail to run water, and a stove, aware of the laws of arts, does not get hot enough to actually fry a pan of bacon and eggs.

The reality of a theatrical production is established by an unspoken agreement on the part of an audience: we will ourselves to believe.

Our will can be served equally well by literal imitation or by conventional symbols. Up to a certain point, our belief that the stage is a world is backed by the imitation of things that are real to us because we come in contact with their counterparts daily. But, no imitation can be complete enough to deceive us. We are always watching a play. Beyond a certain point, we agree to deceive ourselves.

Make-Believe

An element of make-believe can't be separated from the theatre. We cannot accept the first word of any play without saying to ourselves, in effect, "Let's pretend."

A performance in the theatre is obviously make-believe, a mimicking of life. Yet, the lives it portrays often seem to us more real than our own. During every minute we watch actors performing, we know they are dressed up as we once dressed up as children. "Pretending," as we said then, playing at being Kings, Queens, gods, heroes or persons like ourselves. We acknowledge this when we interrupt them to applaud them for acting—that is, pretending, so well.

But, the interruption does not snap the spell. The human beings portrayed can become more real to us than a wife, a friend or child seated at our side. The emotions aroused by an obvious imitation of love or death can be more violent than any we have felt during our own love affairs or our personal losses.

Sometimes this emotion may hit the playgoer on the way out of the theatre, but if it occurs to them in a way that breaks the fourth wall during the performance, the production fails.

Everything on the stage, by the magic that a successful show gets across, becomes what it pretended to be.

At the same time, the theatre, in its effect, is so complete an imitation of life that no degree can destroy its reaction as a picture of existence. No play, however realistic in intention, can ever be wholly so in the theatre.

A dramatic critic may hail a masterpiece, but he knows, like the most illiterate theatregoer, the aged characters are not as old as they seem, the sick and suffering have no actual malady and murder and tests are obvious pretense.

CHAPTER
twenty-three

The Role of the Scene Designer

<u>The Designer as Intermediary</u>

If designers had turned scenery for all poetic plays into uniform serenity, their settings could never have had any relation to a living theatre. Modern scenery has been associated with "art theatres" because these have been born not of an interest in art, in its formal sense, but of an interest in ideas and a widespread conviction that the theatre is, at the moment, suited to reinterpreting life and reconceiving the world.

It is typical that theatre designing rose to the rank of a separate profession, in this country, and "art theatres" like the Washington Square Players, the Province Town Theatres and the Theatre Guild Theatres that were dedicated not to providing visual, beautiful spectacles, but to begin what seemed to be important ideas in terms of dramatic stories.

Stage design is part and parcel of the total effort of interpreting script—an important factor in overcoming the resistance of an audience to dramatic ideas that transcend its stereotyped expectations. But, design is as necessary for staging the excepted masterpieces of the past as it is for plays that are assumed to be masterpieces of the present. The presentation of significant ideas where the theme of a play is based on contemporary material, because of the ideas' relevance, involves a definite struggle with audiences' preconceptions and taboos.

The presentation of the important ideas of the past becomes a struggle to overcome the seeming irrelevance, because the audience is inclined to be not annoyed but indifferent.

The justification for all settings is the total impact. The value and the meaning of each play as performed in modern times when the production was created in the past, may presently seem old-fashioned. Like the long sideburns and the hoop skirts of a past era, what inappropriate raiment for a grand passion!

Prop to Playwriting

Directors are often criticized for depending too much on the scenic background of a play in order to illustrate its meaning. No doubt this happens occasionally, although playwrights often do not realize the full implications of what they have written. But, the increasing emphasis placed upon stage scenery is to not only be the directors' reliance upon it, but to the fact that playwrights themselves use it more and more as a prop to playwriting and depend on the details of the stage setting to do some of the work they formerly had to do entirely with words.

Always let an audience know at a glance, in conjunction with all other details of furnishing, the education, income habits and social class of a leading character. Prepare his entrance much less clumsily than by marking time while an audience listens to a maid and a butler discussing their master and telling each other what they know about him.

Molière's leading characters usually establish position by their costumes, their manners or elaborate verbal explanations of themselves, as well as verbal descriptions of them by the other characters in the play.

But in those days, when costumes would basically be the same, there is so little that can distinguish a high official in a one-button cutaway, from an undertaker wearing a similar type of dress.

Every object on the stage serves not only the immediate purpose of use by the actors, handled or sat upon, but also the ultimate purpose of characterizing a social environment that validates everything the actors do.

Thus, such impersonal things, such as sounds, can have the importance of a dramatic happening; for example, the traditional thunderclap or blinding flash have a carefully plotted and sustained role to play.

Is it an exaggeration to say the details of setting a stage have become an integral part of the technology of playwriting itself?

CHAPTER
twenty-four

Drama in Schools

A few notes are included on the subject of school drama as this aspect of the amateur stage has many particular problems. One of the most important features in this respect is the question of age.

Few children below the age of eleven show any particular talent in dramatics. They may be bursting with enthusiasm during the early stages of a rehearsal, but soon tire of the novelty and make themselves more trouble than they are worth.

It should be remembered in this connection that, although children often show an aptitude for singing and dancing at a much earlier age, these accomplishments are not incredibly hard for them and do not require such sustained effort. There are exceptions to this rule of course, but it is a wise plan to exclude children from important dramatic roles, except for small parts until they are eleven or twelve.

While it may be recognized that the child of ten years is often eager but unable to concentrate, a good deal of change takes place in a period of twelve months. The more sophisticated children of eleven, twelve and thirteen make great advances in the mental sphere, and are much more reliable from the producer's standpoint.

Unfortunately, this ideal cooperation does not last long.

Through adolescence, the years seem fraught with shyness, overconfidence or a strange mixture of both qualities.

With the latter group, the school producer has to contend with new, and sometimes urgent problems. Yet, in spite of this drawback, glimpses of talent may shine through the obstinate exterior.

At ten, children want to try everything new and to change as soon as it becomes familiar. For the next two or three years, they are less impulsive and more amiable, but also less likely to shine in an exceptional manner. When fourteen has been reached, it is usually easier to pick out the good from the bad and indifferent. Even the most gifted young amateurs are liable to have their individual moods and difficult moments.

It may often seem the most talented are also the most troublesome. Whatever pains may be taken on the part of the producer, there is no chance of disguising fact when a young actor has done well.

While such knowledge may spur some to higher efforts, it is more likely the average adolescent will get a swelled head. To do away with this, and other problems, it is a good idea to keep the age groups mixed well. As long as there are no great differences in height, this is one of the main secrets of a successful school drama.

It may be noted; even in this respect, age is usually adjusted to the importance of the part.

The choice of a suitable play is another important matter for youth productions. Most boys and girls study Shakespeare and other traditional masterpieces at school. Reading the parts around the group in a dull manner once or twice a week is typically how this is done. It is not surprising that, in these circumstances, familiarity breeds contempt.

The great dramas have to be acted with every fiber of the mind and body—a task that is far too demanding for the young performer. This does not mean school groups should go to the opposite extreme and shun real character work in favor of silly adventures. It is probable the young actors themselves would be the first to rebel at any attempts to move in this direction.

A better choice would be something like the "Ghost Train" with plenty of excitement and, above all, a modern background. Few girls and even fewer boys get much fun out of creating a past age that they do not understand. Yet, whatever is chosen let it be a classic of its kind, lesser-known works and experiments of doubtful values are well enough left to older people. It is advisable for the promoters of school drama to follow where others lead.

One of the disadvantages of plays in schools is usually the lack of permanent quarters and adequate equipment. This is a setback shared by many groups, but with schools in particular, as space is limited. There is extreme difficulty in finding a suitable place to perform, let alone fitting that space for drama. In some schools the erstwhile theatre is a gymnasium, dining hall or even a large classroom. There are some schools where the children are fortunate enough to have a permanent stage, which may also be the art room, divided from the assembly hall by a folding screen.

Although there are many difficulties to overcome in providing school drama, these should be approached with a spirit of optimism.

Mistakes must be avoided, but allowances are generally made for younger people; however, there are faults of an obvious nature that reflect on all adults concerned with the effort.

There is, for example, no excuse for allowing the area used to remain austere and scholastic. Even school plays should be a source of pleasure and performed in a suitable atmosphere. Those invited to see a gripping thriller or a happy comedy, may well be put off by having to sit on hard benches, or uncomfortable chairs. Make an attempt to provide comfortable seating, even if this has to be obtained from outside vendors.

Evidence that the "theatre for a night" serves more commonplace ends can be hidden beneath colorful hangings. Do everything possible to make the visiting members of the audience feel at home by conducting them to their seats and providing programs.

Above all, warn the lunatic fringe among the pupils to refrain from talking and horseplay. In most schools, the main responsibilities for drama fall on the shoulders of one person. Yet, however knowledgeable such a person may be, it is unfair for him or her to carry the burden alone.

The heads of special departments concerned with art and crafts or musical training are usually capable of cooperation and advice. This should be encouraged at all times, particularly when a stage has to be made out of trestles, or extensive landscape is needed for a backdrop.

It ought to be emphasized in all departments that drama is a school effort, not just the job of a few boys or girls playing roles or operating stage effects. Duties can be shared, and even those not taking a direct part should cooperate by selling tickets and helping with posterior work or publicity.

CHAPTER
twenty-five

Music

It is important that the right music is chosen to assist the general effect, as this can improve or spoil a performance to a considerable extent. In making the final choice, avoid anything that will seem distracting or irrelevant.

Jazz music and popular melodies are unsuitable with a straight play, as they lack the dignity and dramatic tone that the occasion requires. Highly classical works such as chamber music or a movement from a concerto are not recommended, as these are too somber or pretentious for the average production. It may be noted, in this respect, great works draw too much attention to themselves, to the deterrent of other features of the production.

Avoid music the audience might consider ultramodern, or too old fashion. In recent years, there has been a tendency to play harpsichord music as background to any play earlier than the late 19th century or later than the 16th century. Those responsible for such digressions are of the opinion that antique instruments are needed for conveying period atmosphere; however, this idea does not take into account the essential narrative quality of certain types of good music, which may have sound pictures of any shade without the aid of particular instruments.

Although an audience is willing to accept the historical setting and manners of a period play, strange music, often introduced before the curtain rises, may well destroy their confidence. A strident modern accompaniment to a play set in more recent times should be gauged for the same reason. In both cases, people are inclined to feel they are being drawn out of their depths of mental environments. Few would be expected to own as much in actual words, but the inner reaction is present which may breed hostility to other aspects of the production.

After the foregoing reservations, it may seem that the producer's choice of music is very limited; however, when the wealth of material which can be drawn from the works of 19th century or Romantic composers is considered, the matter is seen in its true prospective.

Many of these composers, such as Mendelson's, Nicoli and Grieg, wrote a great deal of theatre music for "A Midsummer Night's Dream," and almost without parallel in this respect may serve as a model for good theatrical music.

As those of the 20th century, with such classics as "Oklahoma," "West Side Story," Man of LaMancha," "Chicago" and many others. Concert overtures and pieces of these kinds are easy to find and popular with most types of audiences.

Regarding the interpretation of playing music, the ideal situation is to cooperate with amateur musicians: sometimes the best alternative is to play amplified records.

While most regular theatres have an orchestra that seems to be part of the theatre-going experience, the band should be fully competent. In all circumstances, recorded music is much better than a third-rate orchestra. If the latter choice is made, care should be taken to avoid an infringement of copyright laws. Record companies who protect the recordings from use on public occasions indicate this fact on the labels of their products.

CHAPTER
twenty-six

Some Well-Known Plays

O pinions may vary according to taste, but taste in its essence is formed by contact with different points of view.

In making a selection from plays by Bernard Shaw, both for their interest and suitability, "Candida" might easily head the popular list. It has, among other attributes, an interesting plot and flowing dialogue. These are typical assets of a play by Shaw, who, with lively and inventive genius, produced many original themes. "Candida" falls into the latter category, but is given a new significance by its original setting.

When it was written, this was probably considered a revolutionary, or at least unusual play; even now it may be thought of as a departure from convention, both in setting and circumstance. From every aspect, this is a triumph of the writer's craft. The main ingenuity of this production lies in the axiom that, "things are not what they seem," and "the mind is a measure of man."

"Twelfth Night" is one of the most amusing of Shakespeare's comedies, and perhaps the best suited for amateurs to perform.

There are no stirring roles in the play as there are in most Shakespearean dramas. The Duke Orsino, Lady Olivia, Viola and her twin brother are more or less conventional parts; however, there are many beautiful lines, especially in the Duke's opening speech, which offers a chance for poetic rendering.

Each of the main characters is able to share the credits of these lines, but it must be felt the most interesting part of this play is the element of buffoonery supplied by many in this play.

"The Rivals"; The Iris seems to have a genius for producing writers of first-class comedy, among them being such giants as Bernard Shaw, Oliver Goldsmith, Oscar Wilde and Richard Sheridan.

In "The Rivals," which many consider Sheridan's masterpiece, we have typical Irish wit. For the modern public, it has the added attraction of representing the 18th century without any of its real squalor and inhumanity.

Members of the audience are moved by a spectacle of stately manners, and beautiful costumes that seem far, in spirit, from wayside gallows and mob riots.

In spite of what may seem an aloofness from the prevailing social conditions, the play is excellent material for both amateurs and professionals. The characters are drawn with such good humor and taste that their apparent isolation is a benefit rather than a discrepancy.

"The Rivals" is what might be termed a formal play in the best sense. Some people may object to the frequent asides and spoken thoughts, but if these are accepted as a period formality, there should be no more objections of a serious nature.

"Peer Gynt" is a play with a departure from those previously discussed, as it is less familiar in setting and more fantastic in theory.

There is plenty of fine material in it for amateurs, but it is better for them to concentrate on various scenes of a modified version. The reason for this being if the play is done in its entirety, there will be far too many problems for most amateur producers and designers. For example, the action moves in stride from a desert coast to a lunatic asylum and then to the deck of a floundering vessel—these problems will appear obvious.

On the credit side, "Peer Gynt" is an excellent example of expressionistic drama, at which Scandinavian writers of the 19th century excelled. It offers plenty of humor, poetry and dramatic scope for play reading. As amateurs should practice in this department, "Peer Gynt" is well worth considering.

I would be remiss if I didn't mention one of the best American plays in recent times, "Death of a Salesman" by Arthur Miller. I am proud to say my wife Vivian and I had the extreme pleasure and honor to play the leads of Linda and Willy Loman in Cheshire, Connecticut. The story of this play is known worldwide, and follows the last days of an ailing traveling salesman who seeks to find out, by a tragic series of soul-searching revelations of the past life he has lived with his wife, his sons and his business associates, just where and how he has failed to win success and happiness.

It is a thrilling work of deep and revealing beauty. "Death of a Salesman" shows man's inhumanity to man and their frailty.

It's a show for amateurs and professionals, as it will touch the souls and hearts of all who see it, as well as those who perform in this masterpiece of American drama.

CHAPTER
twenty-seven

Licensing & Insurance

The local authorities license theatres and music halls throughout the world. If amateurs require the use of a hall or public rooms where plays are not regularly staged, they must acquire a temporary license from the state.

The method of applying for a license may vary from one district to another, and in some parts a justice of the peace grants them.

A license is not required when the play is to be acted as a private performance. This implies the type of show to which friends and subscribers are invited. If tickets are sold for entertainment in this category, they must be obtained in advance and limited to those who are known to the society. Tickets cannot be sold at the door when a performance claims to be private. It must be remembered that exemption from entertainment tax, now extended to all amateurs, does not preclude the need for a license.

Insurance

If the amateur group employs paid assistance, it should be checked to make sure they are covered for insurance, probably under an employer's liability policy. It should be noted those employed without remuneration are not considered within this category. The compensation which an employer (or employers) have to pay in the event of a paid employee becoming injured changes according to the extent of the injury.

Third-party insurance is another form of coverage, which is a wise choice for amateur companies. It concerns accidents to those in the hall or theatre. Most theatres are protected by measures undertaken by the owners, in which case it is not the concern of those who merely rent or borrow the premises for a short period.

Policies may be obtained to cover almost any type of accident, from fire and flood to financial setbacks due to unusual weather. An all-risks or comprehensive policy, although costing more than a limited premium, is the safest method of insurance.

Personal injury covers those who are injured while performing or rehearsing with the company. Such accidents may include a wide range of likely events, from tripping to colliding with sceneshifters. A policy of this kind that would cover the whole cast, to which members contribute equal amounts, is much cheaper than buying individual policies.

Rights and Restrictions

There are a few major publishing houses that cover Canada and the United States of America; they are Samuel French Inc., Dramatic Publishers and Music Theatre International (MTI).

Copyright laws and conventions protect these companies, and therefore it is an infringement of copyright law to give a performance, or reading of any protected play, without consent from the publishing house.

It is also a violation of the copyright law to copy part or all of a play by any means, including type writing, photocopying or videotaping.

Additionally, they are sometimes required to restrict availability of certain productions. Slightly restricted means there are certain times the show is available, and territorial limitations in effect.

Royalties

Royalties listed with each play are for live stage productions by amateur groups with maximum seating capacities of 400. Professional groups, and also amateur groups with larger seating capacities, as well as television and radio broadcasts must make special arrangements. Productions may not be videotaped without prior arrangement. Royalties compensate authors and owners for the use of their works, and are applicable to all performances before an audience—whether or not admission is charged.

When two amounts are listed, or a range of ticket prices is used—such as $60-$90—the first is for the first performance and the second is the royalty for each succeeding performance. Royalties are subject to change without notice.

Production Requirements

Whenever a play is produced, due authorship credit must be given on all programs, printing and advertising. No changes may be made in the text of a play without prior written consent.

Advertising and Publicity

Eye-catching, two-color posters and helpful publicity kits are available for many of the most popular plays and musicals. These provide safe ways to promote the show, as they are pre-approved from the licensing houses.

All that I mentioned can also be applied to the majority of other publishing houses outside of those I named.

CHAPTER
twenty-eight

The Dos & Don'ts of Theatre

In this chapter, we recap some of the key elements, and I offer some final thoughts on behavior and responsibilities regarding theatre.

Upstaging

One of the cardinal rules of theatre, as you may remember, is don't upstage. To refresh, if you are in a scene with another actor, don't draw attention to yourself while someone else is delivering lines or an action.

First of all, it can be very disconcerting to the other actor and could destroy a scene. Another way of upstaging is disregarding the directions given to you by the director during rehearsals. You should always take notes, and write them in pencil, in case of changes, in your script.

Never stand in front of another actor when both of you are conversing your lines, unless the director told you to do this as it has relevance to the character relationships. Not only will it annoy who you are doing this to, you could throw them out of their character or cause them to forget their lines.

Concentration

Whenever you are in a scene with other performers, and you don't have lines or a particular action movement, stay in character and concentrate on whatever is being said or done by those that have lines or movement.

I'll give you a few instances of this bad behavior that I have seen many times during a show when a lack of concentration occurs.

Sometimes performers start looking around the set, or at the audience and even bite their nails or pick their nose—no kidding! Believe me, this can destroy the image a particular scene is depicting, and astute audiences will pick it up without a doubt.

Make sure if you have an entrance to make, you are there on time. It is your responsibility, not anyone else's. I'll give you an example; I had the lead of Willy Loman in "Death of a Salesman," and I was in the middle of a dramatic scene with my sons.

The actor who played my neighbor was supposed to make an entrance, and he didn't, so I did some improvising to give the stage manager time to find him.

When she did, she found that he was trying to make out with one of the women backstage.

Can you believe that?!

Look The Part

Let us say you're involved with a period play, either including a past century or modern day. Make sure you have the proper attire and makeup on. Imagine if you are performing as the king of Siam, or you're part of the court of Siam. All characters should look the part, especially if you don't have lines. This is not only your responsibility, but also the director's, to ensure the makeup and costumes are on point. You should all look Thai, not like you walked in off a street in America.

Lines

Always know your lines by the time you have a dress rehearsal, and well before the opening. The words you say determine who and what you are portraying. Could you imagine if you were doing lines in Act I, Scene Two and suddenly go into Act II, Scene Two? It could be devastating, but if you can retain your character it's easier to recover.

Props

If you have particular props that you have to bring on with your entrance, don't forget them. How would it look if you walked on with a rubber ducky that someone would have used in a comedic bath scene when you should have had a raincoat on and umbrella since the scene called for a rainy day?

Of course I'm being fictitious, but it could happen if you don't pay attention to your entrance.

Stage Fright

This can happen to the amateur or the experienced actor. It is very important you know the story you are in, and the relations with your fellow performers.

By knowing this, you can possibly bail out a fellow actor by staying in character and gently reminding him or her who and what they were doing at the time in a particular scene.

These occurrences can happen on opening night when you are anxious to do something special, or in the middle or end of a long run of the play.

Sometimes a fellow actor may come to you for advice in doing a role. Although you want to be a nice person, do them and yourself a favor by politely speaking to the director about it.

This is what a director is for, as they shape and form the show and characters.

Finally, you must, at all times, be the character you are portraying. Always remember where and what you have to do. You are in a different world on the stage. The audience doesn't exist. They are there to observe and enjoy your performance.

CHAPTER
twenty-nine

The Good

When I came out of the army, my future wife Vivian asked me if I would like to see a show in New York City.

My reply was, "Do you mean a movie?"

She laughed and told me, "No, I mean a Broadway show. They have special price tickets."

You see, I had never seen a theatrical show my whole young life as I was primarily involved with baseball.

Well, we went, the show we saw was "Porgy and Bess." I loved it and we were singing some of the music to each other on the way home in the car. That's when I started to have a passion for theatre, and we saw many shows after that.

About six years later when we bought our first home in Commack, New York, I was bowling with my friend Saul when out of the blue he said, "Jay, why don't you and I start a theatre here?"

I looked at him in shock, and asked, "What did you say?"

He repeated his remark.

"What the hell do I know about theatre?" I replied.

Saul said he studied theatre in college so he would direct, and because I was in sales I could be the producer.

I laughed, paused and then said, "OK, it's a challenge and I don't back away from a challenge."

So, we went to work. We selected as our first show, Neil Simon's "Come Blow Your Horn."

I went around and got some space at Beth David, the local synagogue, got a stage, 20' x 16' as the show would be done in the round, contacted someone in the beauty business and got makeup donated to us. Also, I arranged for local people, including us, to lend furniture, and as far as costumes, each actor would use their own outfits.

Saul cast the show, and we had five weeks before we opened. A couple of days before we had the read-through by the cast, Saul informed me he had to leave town on business and I could run the read-through.

About twenty minutes before I left, I got a call from the person who was playing the lead role. He told me, "I understand we rehearse three days a week."

Which, in today's standard of five or six days a week, is nothing.

He continued, "I have two of those days that I play tennis."

I replied with a loud, "What?" as I tried to remain calm. I told him that I would be leaving for the read-through shortly and advised him to take five minutes and call me back with his final decision as to which he would choose. He called and didn't change his mind. I replied, as producer, that he was out of the show and we would recast the role. When I got to the theatre, I told the cast what had happened and updated them we would recast the role as soon as Saul got back.

I said to them I would read his part for continuity's sake that evening.

At the end of the reading, there was dead silence.

I thought to myself, "Oh boy, I really screwed up."

Then, the actor who had the lead role as the father approached me, gently grabbed my collar and said, "You are a natural. We all want you to do this role. Don't recast or we are all quitting."

My knees turned to jelly even if I didn't show it.

Saul got back the next day and I told him what happened.

His reply, as he laughed, "You are no actor."

I agreed with him.

The only acting I ever did was in second year after kindergarten as a carrot in a vegetable patch.

Since he continued to challenge me, I told him to listen to me read and if he wanted to recast we would. After completing the second read-through, Saul came to me and said, "They are right. You have to do this role."

The role of Alan Baker, the lead, had forty-three pages of dialogue. I went home and told Vivian that I was now the lead role. She didn't laugh as she always supported me, but she kindly told me, "I had some theatre experience in college and in high school." So with her help, and my determination, we did the show.

That was a big success, and Vivian even did a walk on for two lines near the end of the show.

Buoyed by the success, we selected Woody Allen's "Don't Drink The Water" as our next play. Vivian had the lead of Marion Hollander, and I had a main supporting role as Father Drobny. It was the first time I used a dialect of Middle Eastern Europe.

I was the only Catholic in a country of 4,999 atheists.

Another big success.

Thus, my theatrical career was launched.

Shortly after the show, my company transferred me to the New England upper New York region. I said my goodbyes reluctantly, but knew I had to go. After I left, I got word the person who played my father had a severe heart attack and passed away. I returned and convinced all in charge to name the theatre in his honor. Thus, the "Sy Siegel Theatre" was born, and as far as I know it is still operating.

After moving to Cheshire, Connecticut, I got involved with the local theatre. The theatre was going to hold auditions for the play "Our Town" by Thorton Wilder.

It takes place in a small New Hampshire town. Of course, the characters would require a northeastern accent. I went to read for the storyteller, who sets all the scenes and more or less tells the story as it unfolds.

I have the ability to do dialects, so before I read I asked the director if I should read it in the character voice or my own, which is New York by nature.

She told me to do it in my regular voice. I did and didn't get the part. It was given to a friend of the director.

The play was being produced in the local high school stage, which was about forty-five feet deep and fifty some odd feet across. They offered me a small part as the constable Bill Warren who was 90 years old. Since I love the story, I accepted the role.

I had to play it at the back end of the stage, and we didn't have microphones. Well, I did it with a perfect New Hampshire accent. When the reviews came out in *The Waterbury Times*, the main paper in our area, much to my surprise they featured my role as the most authentic role, and clearest voice in the whole show.

All I had were four pages of dialogue whereas the person that was given the lead was hardly mentioned. You can only imagine how I felt, as I was truly the character I portrayed.

It's not always important what role you do, as long as you're doing it well. All these experiences were good, and I am thankful to all those people who got me to do theatre that I love!

CHAPTER
thirty

The Bad

There are times the sun doesn't always shine; there are days when dark clouds will be over us.

So it is true with theatre as well.

There was a time at a repertory theatre in New Britain Connecticut when Vivian and I had the leads in "Night of January 16th" by Ayn Rand.

I played John G. Whitfield and Vivian played a Swedish character Magda Svenson.

Well we had this very young male director, who would walk around with a 2 x 4 in his hand. Every time he'd make a point, or if he didn't like something, he would bang this piece of wood on the stage. After some time, it was getting very disconcerting, and all of us were getting quite annoyed.

Finally, one day during a rehearsal one of the cast members asked me, as the lead, to tell him to stop or they would walk out.

Now having been a director myself, I try not to tell another director what to do; however, this had to be addressed. So, I took him aside where we could have a private talk.

At first, he was very belligerent towards me. Finally, I told him if he did not stop, and also get rid of the piece of wood, I would put it where the sun doesn't shine.

I also advised him the cast would walk out of the show.

We had only three weeks before opening.

Well, he got rid of the 2 x 4 and apologized to the entire cast.

I just don't know which threat worked.

HA!

There was this time I had the lead role of Carmine Vespucci in "The Ritz," a play by Terrance McMalley. I played this comical mafia chieftain who had tracked down his brother-in-law in a gay bathhouse. Since he had insulted my sister (his wife) and treated her badly, I was going to take him out.

This show was done at a professional theatre in Hartford Connecticut and the center of the stage was on a revolve.

As I was in this scene with other people in the bathhouse, I heard a loud crack. As I looked up, I saw that one of the main walls was starting to separate.

Staying in character, I went to the wall and leaned against it to prevent it from coming down. I stayed there for the entire scene.

As the act ended, the director came running up to me screaming, "You were supposed to move down stage!"

I stopped him, took him to the wall and showed him the tear. He had tech do an emergency repair and didn't even thank me or apologize to me.

Oh well!

I performed in "Oliver!", inspired by Charles Dickens' classic, at a repertory theatre in New Britain Connecticut. I did three roles: rich man, poor man and the iconic character of Mr. Sowerberry the undertaker.

As Sowerberry, I had this song to sing as I walked around a coffin. I worked extremely hard on this show, as I had three quick changes and extreme makeup to put on as the undertaker.

The actress who played my wife was the sister of the director. She didn't like the way I was singing the comical song and went to her sister and asked the song be taken away from me.

We opened the next night.

I told her it wasn't very nice to go behind my back to the director, and she simply laughed and walked away.

Now, the scene with the coffin required for her to get in the casket as I walked around it. Well, instead of walking around it, I sat on it through the whole scene, in character.

She was banging to get out, and no way until I finished the scene was she going to.

Talk about sweet revenge!

I was in rehearsals for the "Cocktail Hour" at a community theatre in Arizona. I had this obnoxious woman who played my daughter. At rehearsals, she would constantly upstage me by standing in front of me and blocking me.

I tried to talk to her, but she was what you call a "know it all." Besides, the director was a friend of hers.

I made the best of it, by moving to the side of her every time she was upstaging me.

There was this scene where I have an argument with my son and storm off into the wings. The area is dark and you cannot see too clearly. This one particular day, as I ran off into the wings, I smacked into two music stands made of metal, which held two glasses of water and two open bottles. I fell to the floor, scraped my knee and banged my elbow.

I found out later this same woman and her friend had left it there.

There was now water all over the floor.

I ran to the back room to get some paper towels to wipe it up, but there weren't enough towels, and I had to be back onstage in two more pages of dialogue.

At the end of the scene, I went to the lobby of the theatre to get more towels. As I was walking up the aisle, the woman come screaming out to center stage hollering at me, "I was brought up that when you make a mess you clean up the mess, but apparently some people weren't brought up properly."

I was steaming.

She and her friend had created the situation. I finished the act and left. By the way, the director didn't say anything.

That night, I called the president of the theatre and told her unless I had an apology I would not be returning. Now I had a lead, and we were two weeks away from opening night.

The president ignored me, as she didn't want to say anything to this obnoxious woman. I tried three times to get her to apologize, as I was treated very badly through no fault of my own.

It was to no avail, so I left the show and never worked for this theatre again.

I enjoy theatre, but when you are treated in that manner you have to stand up for yourself if no one else well.

It was the first and only time I walked out of a show.

I am not suggesting anyone do this as common practice, but if you have to work in a bad environment, it is best not to work in a situation such as this.

One last thought: I had the lead of Nat Miller in "Ah, Wilderness" by Eugene O'Neill. It was the only comedy that he had written. There was this actor who did the role of Sid Davis, my wife Essie's brother in the play.

The actor would show up inebriated, and would either slur his lines or would throw off any actor during a scene with him.

We were getting close to the opening, and myself as well as some of the other actors went to the director to ask him to straighten this guy out or replace him. He told us he would speak to him, and, for a few days, things got better.

Unfortunately though, this man fell into his old ways once again.

The night we opened, I noticed the actor was drinking out of a bottle that appeared to look like beer. When I approached him and said, "I hope that isn't a bottle of beer," he told me it was water.

During the opening scene, I was in the dining room at the table with my show family talking. My back was turned when I heard lots of laughter. Now I know this scene wasn't intended to be funny.

Finally, I turned around and saw this character Sid Davis come onstage drunk, he even put red makeup on his nose and had his jacket hanging loosely over his shoulder.

I got up, retaining my character, grabbed him firmly by his arm and sat him down in a chair. I told one of the kids playing my son to keep him there during the whole scene.

After that, the director assigned someone to check him out before each show.

Some people will never learn, oh well.

Now to something beautiful!

CHAPTER
thirty-one

The Beautiful

As I mentioned, Vivian and I performed in the classic play "Death of a Salesman" in Connecticut. As you now know, Arthur Miller, one of the best storytellers, wrote the play.

We played the leads – Linda and Willy Loman. It wasn't an easy show, as at the time I was a salesman and had to spend a lot of time out of town.

It was one of the most emotional plays either one of us had done, especially together. In the audience was a young man who was recording the show. I still have the tape today. On the tape you can hear this young man sobbing as he got into the play.

Oh, by the way, that young man is my beloved son Richard.

Unbeknownst to us, the theatre got in touch with Arthur Miller, as he lived in Connecticut at that time. He was invited to see the production, and ended up coming!

Although he didn't come backstage at the end of the show because it would have caused all kinds of chaos being the private person that he was, he did request the director to get our scripts. He then signed our script covers, and also wrote a note to us with fabulous remarks:

To Vivian and Jay Horne, the Lomans:

This was one of the finest productions of my show. You both played your characters as I had written them to be. Congratulations.

Sincerely,
Arthur Miller

Now let me go back to a play I mentioned in another chapter, "The Ritz." If you recall, it took place mainly in a gay bathhouse. I was the comical villain who distained the people in the bathhouse, as I was out to get my brother-in-law.

Throughout most of the play, I only wore a T-shirt, underwear, black garter belts on my legs and a snub-nosed 38-pistol tucked into my underwear or the garter belt.

One Saturday night, the theatre did a benefit for the Gay Church of Hartford Connecticut, so the entire audience was gay, including some of the actors in the show. As you know, it is a tradition in theatre at the end of the show for the actors to come out for a curtain call.

Since I had the lead, I came out last. All that preceded me received loud applause, and now it was my turn. It started with this hissing sound followed by loud "boo's" and laughter.

What a compliment! It was an absolute affirmation as to my character depiction, which is the ultimate reward for a performer.

I have played a priest three times, as I mentioned. The second was a comic version in "Don't Drink the Water."

The two other times were in "Mass Appeal" by Bill C Davis. The first time I did the role was in Ridgefield Connecticut, then in Sherman New York. Both were repertory theatres, or semi-professional.

I'd like to talk about the first time I did the role of Father Tim Farley in Ridgefield. Not being of the Catholic faith, this was quite a challenge for me. I had to give thirteen masses during the play, and there was only one other character with me, a young seminarian.

What I did to learn about the role was attend St. Mary's Church in Ridgefield every Sunday to study how Father John conducted the masses, and what he did as a leader of his parish.

After a few Sunday visits, I introduced myself to Father John, and we became quite friendly as he advised me in how to present myself in the show. In fact, he lent me many of his outfits.

I invited Father John to come and see the show. He took me up on the offer and one Saturday night he came with many of his young seminarians in tow.

At the end of the show, he met me outside the theatre. I was curious as to how he enjoyed the show, and asked if I did him proud playing this priest.

His response, "Jay, my son, let me ask you a question."

I remarked, "Of course. What is it? Did I do something wrong?"

He replied, "Not at all. I was thinking of taking off a Sunday, what are you doing two Sundays from now?"

"Actually nothing," I replied, "the show will end in two weeks."

"Fine," he replied, "I would like for you to fill in for me. Your performance was so believable some of my seminarians thought you were the real thing."

I laughed, thanked him and shook his hand.

That's one of the finest compliments I've ever received from a performance.

There was a time I was directing "The Miracle Worker" by William Gibson. It's the story of the deaf and blind Helen Keller and her nurse Annie Sullivan.

At the audition, there were many young girls and boys. For the role of Helen, I had a test for them. I placed an old satchel on the stage that contained dolls and some toys. I lead them onto the stage, with eyes closed, and placed them by the satchel to see what they would do.

Many of them opened the satchel and started to tell me what they felt. Then came along this young girl about nine or ten years old with long brown hair. She knelt down, acted scared and didn't talk. She opened the satchel and threw away some of the dolls.

This was my Helen.

Prior to rehearsal, I took all of the young children, including the person playing Helen and the one that would do the role of Annie Sullivan, to the Blind Institute in Hartford Connecticut so they could mingle with children that were blind, and some deaf as well.

The nurse and doctors thanked me for coming and caring for those that needed people to pay them a visit. At the end of one of our shows we were surprised by a visit as well, as some of the doctors and nurses from the Institute had attended.

They asked if they could address the cast, and entire artistic team.

One of the nurses and a doctor spoke to us. In essence, they said, "You all have presented with this show, that if you have a defect such as blindness or are deaf, that you should care that those such people are human beings, too. Human beings who are just trying to reach out and get help. Thank you for having this wonderful show."

There wasn't a dry eye in the cast after they spoke, including my own.

Finally, there was this time I played the character of an old sailor called Salty Dog. It was for American Family Insurance, and the show was called "Legend of Pirates Cove." We performed it in Puerto Rico in a ballroom that held 1,500 people.

We told the story of how American Family Insurance got started many years ago, when pirates were around. For the role, I grew a very itchy beard. Salty Dog told the story, as other performers did the scenes while I was talking.

At the end of the show, I couldn't wait to get back to my room to shave off the beard; however, in order to get to my room I had to go through many public areas.

Admirers that saw the show constantly stopped me to say how much they enjoyed my realistic performance. When they stopped me, they would say, "We recognize that beard!" Some even asked me to sign their programs.

Wow. Maybe I should have kept the beard, but I knew if Vivian saw me like that she wouldn't let me in the house!

These, ladies and gentlemen, were all special and beautiful memories.

Remember, there are always the good, the bad and the beautiful in all of our lives. Just enjoy every moment you have.

Hopefully you will make theatre a part of your moments now, whether you are involved or simply going to see a production.

-Jay

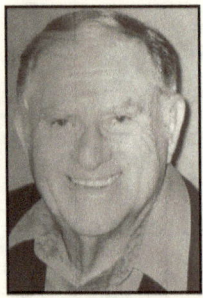

www.ingramcontent.com/pod-product-compliance
Lightning Source LLC
Chambersburg PA
CBHW021410170526
45164CB00002B/582